Syriza

Syriza

Inside the Labyrinth

Kevin Ovenden

Foreword by Paul Mason

Newcastle,
Sept. 2015

First published 2015 by Pluto Press
345 Archway Road, London N6 5AA

www.plutobooks.com

British Library Cataloguing in Publication Data
A catalogue record for this book is available from the British Library

ISBN 978 0 7453 3686 2 Paperback
ISBN 978 1 7837 1696 8 PDF eBook
ISBN 978 1 7837 1698 2 Kindle eBook
ISBN 978 1 7837 1697 5 EPUB eBook

Typeset by Stanford DTP Services, Northampton, England
Text design by Melanie Patrick
Simultaneously printed in the European Union and United States of America

Dedicated to the memories of

Pavlos Fyssas (1979–2013)
and
Shahzad Luqman (1986–2013)

zindabad, ζουν – they live

Contents

Series Preface

The first Left Book Club (1936–48) had 57,000 members at its peak, distributed 2 million books, and had formed 1,200 workplace and local groups engaging in cultural and political activity, including solidarity work (e.g. with Spain), political agitation (against appeasement) and much else. The LBC became an educational mass movement, remodelling British public opinion, and was thought to have been a major factor in the Labour landslide of 1945 and the construction of the welfare state. Publisher Victor Gollancz, the driving force, saw the LBC as a movement against poverty, fascism, and the growing threat of war. He aimed to resist the tide of austerity and appeasement, and to present radical ideas for progressive social change in the interests of working people. The Club was about enlightenment, empowerment and collective organisation.

The world today faces a crisis on the scale of the 1930s. Capitalism is trapped in a long-term crisis due to the dominance of finance over production and austerity programmes, causing suffering, shrinking demand and widening social inequalities, which are tearing apart the social fabric. International relations are increasingly tense and militarised – notably in the Middle East and Eastern Europe – with the danger of war. Neo-fascist and racist groups are gaining ground across much of Europe. Global warming threatens the planet and the whole of humanity with climate catastrophe. Workplace organisation has been weakened, and social democratic parties have been hollowed out by acceptance of pro-market dogma. Society has become more atomised, with politics suffering through peoples' widespread alienation from the system. Yet the last decade has seen historically unprecedented levels of participation in street protest, implying a mass audience for progressive policies. But socialist ideas are no longer, as they were in the immediate post-war period, 'in the tea'. One of neoliberalism's achievements has been to undermine ideas of solidarity, collective provision and public service.

Relaunching the Left Book Club will help us rise to the challenge posed by the global crisis. We will provide a series of high-quality books at affordable prices, published by Pluto Press. Our list will represent a full range of progressive traditions, perspectives and ideas. It will also include reprints of classic texts where appropriate. We hope the books will be used as the basis of reading circles, discussion groups, and other educational and cultural activities relevant to developing, sharing and disseminating ideas for progressive social change in the interests of working people.

The Left Book Club collective

Foreword

Paul Mason

One of our friends in the café, crying. The primary school kids she works with have started to draw euros, cut them out and take them home for their mothers. 'All they hear on the TV, and at home, is about euros, and the lack of money,' she says.

It's the second week of the eurozone's economic blitz on Greece. Medicines, hospital disposables and imported meat are flashing red in the supply chain systems. The banks are closed. Businesses are going bust. But 61 per cent of Greek people have just voted to defy the onslaught and carry on resisting.

It is already clear the eurozone is determined – as the German magazine *Stern* put it – to 'smash Greece'. It would take them two more weeks to force the government into unwilling submission. But the people did not submit.

Another friend, a woman in a fashion business, told her bosses she was voting No in the referendum. 'Don't come in again,' they told her. Another, who works for a magazine, arrived at work before the referendum to find an envelope placed on everybody's desk, containing a ballot paper pre-marked with a Yes vote. The entire workforce voted No.

In the run-up to the referendum every private TV channel ran wall-to-wall propaganda for Yes. It was, for many, the final straw – tipping the waverers over to No during that fateful weekend.

The 5 July referendum, and the imposed third memorandum that followed, marked a turning point both for Syriza and Greece. It demonstrated – not just to Greeks but to the wider left and centre left of Europe – that the eurozone has become a German construct: a game rigged in favour of creating jobs in Germany and destroying them in a broad arc from Lisbon to Thessaloniki.

It demonstrated for the third time in two years the cruel power central banks can wield in a financialised capitalism where the ability to lift a spoon to your baby's mouth depends on the whim of a committee whose arguments are not minuted, whose votes are not explained. The Greek economy was choked close to death by the European Central Bank's refusal to extend emergency lending – and there was no court, no higher body to which the victims of this medieval-style siege warfare could appeal.

On the night Syriza won the election, 25 January 2015, I sat in Athens with journalists who had covered the election at the grassroots, numb: unable to face going to the Tsipras victory rally. We knew at some point this mass enthusiasm and hope would clash with the dour reality of a Europe designed for stagnation and economic servitude. We all knew we had a duty to document this – and Kevin Ovenden's book fulfils that duty superbly.

We don't know, yet, the full story. But the virtue of writing swiftly a comprehensive first draft of the events is that the filter of ideology, subsequent revelation, and future political allegiances cannot be applied. It is as close to the truth as one person's eyes and brain can take us. There will be other versions, and a bigger truth will emerge, but the story Ovenden narrates follows the same arc as the one I lived through.

There was the surge of hope during the election, where all the modernising forces in Greece clustered around Alexis Tsipras, shattering the impetus of the coalition parties. Tiny villages in the mountains, which had voted for the oligarchic parties for decades, swung to Syriza by margins in excess of the overall 36 per cent poll result.

Then there was Varoumania. Yanis Varoufakis emerged late into the narrative of Syriza and even now, in August 2015, facing a politicised prosecution attempt, his personality mesmerises the global media to an extent that obscures what really happened. Varoumania began on the day he 'killed the Troika' in a tetchy meeting with his

Dutch counterpart Jeroen Dijsselbloem in Brussels and ended on 20 February with Syriza being forced to abandon 70 per cent of its election programme.

Then there was what seems, in retrospect, a long, hypnotic period in which protests subsided, social movements lay dormant, and Syriza struggled to make any of its remaining policies stick. I've seen, from the inside, ministries run with only politicians and political advisers, the civil servants sidelined because they were suspected of acting for the opposition, or for Germany itself.

Like Bolivian president Evo Morales, whom I met during the first period of his time in office, Syriza at times felt like prisoners in these ministries. By contrast, on the streets, the ministers were hailed as heroes. You can only understand what it meant for Varoufakis to be mobbed by well-wishers in the May Day crowd if you consider that, after mid 2011, no minister could be interviewed on the street in Athens. For the pro-Troika politicians after the second memorandum, life had become a world of bodyguards, shuttered offices and secret tunnels.

Ovenden's book captures – as very few news reports have captured – the atmosphere of this fascinating interregnum and the shock of what replaced it: the 'rupture', which, when it came, stunned many who had believed that Syriza in power would never decisively resist the creditors.

Ovenden is one of a small, unlikely group of British journalists – drawn from the left and the unorthodox right – who have tried to cut through stereotypes and ignorance to tell the story of the Greek resistance. As such, he will be pilloried with the stock insult applied to all of us: that we are re-treads of Lord Byron, drawn to this hot-tempered country out of a shallow and simplistic romanticism.

Kevin's book itself is the best response to that. It is the story of a society part destroyed by callous neoliberal doctrine, by a Germany whose elite has become unembarrassed by the prospect of economic warfare against a country where it once planted the Swastika. It is the story of a generation who thought they had left behind the world that produced the civil war, the torture, detention and suffering of their grandfathers – only to see the same political forces take to the streets, and to the twittersphere, with the veiled threat of right-wing violence.

And the story is not over. It took the *faux*-left blogosphere less than a month to swing from lauding Tsipras as a hero to denouncing him as a traitor. Seen at street level, which is always this book's vantage point, he is neither. The real heroes and heroines are the people – who defied their own TV stations and the central bank that tried to starve them, and will now do so in different ways.

The six-month experiment of left government within the neoliberal eurozone ended in strategic retreat and climbdown. For the European left this is a crossroads moment: not only will it likely lead to a swift reappraisal of the euro project, but the experience contains object lessons in the relationship of political parties to mass movements.

Syriza won because it captured the imagination of a wide section of young people abandoned by all other parties, and whose future the eurozone authorities had cancelled without explanation or apology.

It lost because it ran into a hitherto unrecognised force: naked economic war prosecuted by Germany – aided and abetted by tiny nations in East Europe whose populations have spent much of the past century in thrall to despotism.

No mass movement in Greece alone would have been strong enough to defeat what Europe did in July 2015. And Syriza did not consistently mobilise it. And the movement itself distrusted Syriza, or created distance and autonomy from Syriza that will now seem justified to some.

But the movement remains – and by this I mean the micro-level radicalisation of people who are in all other ways ordinary: the nursery teacher, the fashion designer, the magazine guys, the migrant shopkeeper. In the week before the referendum even hardened cynics from the anarchist left, who thought the barricade days of 2008 could not return, would sniff the air on the Oxi (No) demonstrations and say 'This smells interesting.'

That, plus the unworkability of the third bailout without massive debt relief, and the violent subtext in the rhetoric of the right, should be a cause for concern to everybody who wants to see a peaceful, socially just resolution to the crisis Europe has created in Greece.

All we can be sure of, as this book goes to press, is that the crisis is not over and nor is the debate over the future strategy of the European left and social movements.

Preface

'The atmosphere is a little similar to the time after 1968 in Europe.'

Former Polish prime minister Donald Tusk, by then co-president of the European Union (EU), voiced his anxiety to the *Financial Times* on 16 July 2015 about a 'political contagion' spreading from Greece and infecting the continent of Europe as had radical movements of the left in the late 1960s. He continued, 'I can feel, maybe not a revolutionary mood, but something like widespread impatience. When impatience becomes not an individual but a social experience of feeling, this is the introduction for revolutions.'

The most extraordinary aspect of Tusk's warning of a 'spectre haunting Europe'[1] was its timing. The centre-right politician rang the alarm at the 'dangerous idea that there is an alternative' to the official consensus of austerity Europe not at that moment back in January 2015 when the first government of the radical left since the Second World War was elected in Europe – Syriza in Greece. Instead, he expressed his fears in the week when that government surrendered to the demand to sign up to a further package of austerity measures and drove them through the Greek parliament. The government of Alexis Tsipras had given the continent's business and political elites what they wanted. Why then was Tusk warning of virulent, political contagion and sounding like a modern-day Laocoön, the Trojan priest who warned 'I fear the Greeks, even when they bear gifts'?

Part of the answer was provided by Germany's Angela Merkel. She had been central to six months of war minus the shooting to destabilise and defang the Syriza-led government. That week a video clip of her went viral. In it she reduces a 14-year-old Palestinian girl, Reem, in the depressed east German city of Rostock to floods of tears. Reem was to be deported. But you must understand, explained the iron chancellor, that there are thousands of people who we must refuse entry to – and she cited the tens of thousands in the black hole of refugee camps in Lebanon.[2]

So great was the popular outrage at Merkel's callousness that the German government felt forced to relent and allow Reem to stay. But the damage to the ideology of a liberal, democratic and progressive 'official Europe' had already been done. A weeping child refugee and an oblivious world leader struck me at the time as the kind of image which would – or at least should – be etched on Merkel's political tombstone. The 'water-boarding' and 'crucifixion'[3] of Greece and its government had ripped away the façade of a civilised Europe to reveal an ugly face of corporate and elite power. Speaking in parliament in favour of accepting a deal which he acknowledged was terrible, Greek prime minister Alexis Tsipras drew attention to the cracks which had appeared within and between the Troika of institutions – the International Monetary Fund (IMF), the EU and the European Central Bank – which had forced their terms upon Athens.

Though this book argues for an alternative path to the one Tsipras chose in July, he was right about that. It was not a Pyrrhic victory. But the humiliation of the Greek government at the hands of the masters of the eurozone and EU had cost them dear. That was evident in Greece, where the division of the country into two camps – the working-class and popular layers versus the wealthy elites – was greater in July than when Syriza was elected six months earlier. The political polarisation was sharper too – with the parties of the left still eclipsing those of the right and of the old order. Elsewhere in Europe, and despite a constant media barrage against 'lazy Greeks', sympathy for and understanding of those at the sharp end of the worst economic crisis in Europe since the 1930s had grown. It was more widespread than the ranks of the left, who had followed with great enthusiasm the January election campaign. Just one example – in late June a young English guy set up a crowd-funding campaign to raise €1.6 billion, to cover the debt that month which Greece owed the IMF. Within days 100,000 people had pledged an average of €18 each.[4]

That widespread sympathy showed signs of changing the terms of the debate about austerity and Europe – even in Britain, where it had often felt as if to criticise the EU was in some way to line up with a xenophobic right. One organised expression of that shift was the mushrooming in early summer of protests and other events in solidarity with the resistance in Greece to what felt like a coup by the powers that be, if not violently to remove the Greek government then at least to usurp the people's choice expressed democratically in an election.[5]

So, as this book was completed – precisely six months into Syriza taking office – the hope which had greeted its election had not been extinguished. There had been some bitter experiences. But, as the Troika closed in over the summer to demand yet further surrender, the popular and political forces which had produced a stunning electoral victory for the left were far from exhausted.

This book seeks to tell the story both of those six months and of the rise of Syriza as a party of the radical left. In so doing it tries to illustrate the major strategic debates that experience has animated about the future of progressive politics and of the left. The thread it tries to uncover in the recent history of Greece is what I call a 'truly radical' politics. It is politics which is radical not just in the principles and policies of a party which expresses it but in its form – arising from and placing at the centre of political change the collective struggles, the social movements, which have rocked Greek society for the last seven years. It suggests that there is a path between two commonplace assessments on the left of that experience. The first may be called an anti-political (certainly anti-party) 'movementism'. It broadly holds that struggles and campaigns must avoid engaging in the political sphere – especially with elections and political parties – or they will become contaminated and turned into instruments of politicians and establishment interests. It is rather like the advice to underground bands not to sign with a label or they will end up 'going mainstream' and their music losing its edge. The other pole is to see the social movements of masses of people as incapable of bringing change through their own struggles and requiring a party to represent them and change things for them. The mobilisation of people then becomes support for a party in government, which is the central agent of progress.

Those are rather simplistic descriptions of poles in a web of debates about the strategy of movements and parties of the left which go back over a century. Some readers may recognise the echoes of the arguments in the German socialist movement before the First World War or internationally following it. They may even wonder why those earlier debates are not referenced and made explicit. The omission is deliberate. It is not because I think that those debates throughout the last century are anachronistic or have somehow been rendered redundant. I do not. It is rather that this book was written with the 100,000 people prepared to give €18 to end the social disaster in Greece in mind. In the course of writing it, 250,000 people marched in London against David Cameron's austerity Tory government. Some 80,000 took part in Dublin in a demonstration against unfair charges for water. The Greek flag was festooned from beginning to end as Irish victims of austerity policies identified with their counterparts in the European country furthest from them.

So I have sought to avoid the technical language and historical references in those rich earlier debates and instead to illustrate them in, I hope, a popular and accessible way through the Greek experience. That does mean delving into the turbulent history of modern Greece, which is largely unfamiliar – including to most left-wing activists. And, therefore, I also hope that those who perhaps have settled and definite opinions, drawing on their own reading of the history of the left elsewhere, will find themselves challenged to see whether those are borne out by the Greek experience.

The idea for this book and the very possibility of it being written came from my great friend Mark Perryman. It was his idea for me to go to Athens in January to report on the snap election campaign which brought Syriza to power. In a typically practical act of solidarity – to the movement in Greece and to me personally – Mark and the Philosophy Football social enterprise he is part of produced a T-shirt with the legend 'Syriza – Greek for hope', proceeds from the sales of which enabled me to send back daily dispatches from the historic campaign. Mark's enthusiasm and encouragement, amplified by two other friends at Philosophy Football, Hugh Tisdale and Jacquie Rich, saw me beyond January and into the following months in Greece – with the odd road trip thrown in – during which I wrote the book. I am deeply grateful to all three. The meaning of the model of progressive culture and political solidarity they have developed is something I plan to explore more fully at a later date.

David Castle, my editor, was a permanent source of expert advice, encouragement and, above all, patient support. Without him, quite simply, the book would not have been written but itself would have disappeared into the labyrinthine twists and turns it tries to navigate. Sophie Richmond skilfully edited the copy and made many helpful suggestions. Melanie Patrick managed the design of the cover, which I am very proud of. Robert Webb saw through production on an incredibly tight schedule. And Emily Orford championed the book from the beginning, promoting it with great energy. Thanks to them, and to all at Pluto.

I was utterly delighted, if a little daunted, when the directors of the new incarnation of the famed Left Book Club of the 1930s chose this title as their first offering to members. It is a privilege to be so associated with what promises to be a major contribution to the spread of progressive ideas and culture to a wide audience. Neil Faulkner and Anna Minton scrupulously read the first draft. I have taken up many of their suggestions and believe they have strengthened the work in content and style.

I first came to Greece on a school trip in 1983 and have followed Greek politics, culture and society ever since. Sadly, my classics teacher back then who arranged for me to be able to go, Gerald

'Ephraim Nektarios' Thompson, passed away before this book was published. For ten years as a journalist I covered events in Greece and the Balkans. Many Greek friends from then and over the years have given me what understanding I have of its social and political realities. None more so than Thanasis Kampagiannis over these last ten.

Many of the explosive events of the last decade directly reported in the book we participated in or witnessed together. And we discussed every page of it – the history, the politics and the judgements offered. Despite the great responsibility and demands of being one of the anti-fascist movement's lawyers in the historic trial of Golden Dawn (set to last a further year) Thanasis has provided constant support and the most acute political insight, without which nothing of value would have been written.

Over two years ago we took part together in a protest which remains seared into my brain – the 'Athens Anti-fascist City' mobilisation on 19 January 2013. It had been called months beforehand to rally a movement against the neo-Nazis of Golden Dawn. Two nights before it took place, two Golden Dawn thugs stabbed Pakistani retail worker Shahzad Luqman to death in a racist attack. He had worked in Greece for six years, sending back remittances to his elderly parents and siblings. We joined the janaza funeral rites, which took place outside the Athens city hall before the mourners merged *en masse* with the angry anti-fascist demonstration. There was then not one legally permitted mosque in Athens. Close by is an artwork bearing the famous adage of the ancient philosopher Isocrates: 'He is Greek who shares our education (or culture).' Shahzad sold goods in Greek to Greeks on a Greek market stall – he was, by any reasonable definition, Greek. Thanasis represented his family in the successful court action against the murderers and toured Greece with Shahzad's parents, who were like lions in the fight for justice for their son.

The demonstration in January ended in Syntagma Square with a concert. The radicalisation of young Greece was reflected in the crisis years in music. A few weeks later I heard Pavlos Fyssas perform, a really talented and joyous anti-racist rapper. Just eight months later – on 17 September 2013 – he too was stabbed to death by Golden Dawn, in Keratsini, western Athens. The anti-fascist eruption which followed forced the authorities finally to prosecute Golden Dawn as a criminal conspiracy. Pavlos's case is at the centre of the ongoing trial.

So this book is dedicated to the memory of two young Greek men – one of Pakistani heritage. Their murders in the crisis years stand as a permanent warning: if the forces of the left cannot find a way out for society from austerity, racism and war, then lurking in the labyrinth are creatures every bit as monstrous as the Minotaur of ancient myth.

CHAPTER ONE

Between Things Ended and Things Begun

'We won. I actually don't know how I feel: we've never won before.'

With eyes moistening, retired pharmacist Dimitris Vassos spoke for many of his generation of the left as crowds gathered in the early hours in the centre of Athens to hear Syriza leader Alexis Tsipras make his victory speech. Throughout the night votes coming in from the big cities to the islands inched towards an historic victory for the forces of the left, whose forebears had gone through civil war, exile, exclusion from public life and violence at the hands of the state and of the shadowy forces connecting it to the far right. Under Greece's proportional electoral system the tally of Syriza MPs in the 300-seat parliament started ahead, stayed ahead and crept towards the 151 seat threshold for an absolute majority. It was tantalisingly close. But by the small hours as I sat with friends urging on the total with single-figure vote totals from the most remote hamlets flashing across the screen the final result became clear – 149 seats.

Texts and online messages from friends across Europe seemed more perturbed that the radical left had fallen just two seats short of an absolute majority than any of my long-standing friends in Greece. One Greek journalist colleague, with whom I had shared assignments in the Balkans, remarked with good humour and mock exasperation, 'I hope people abroad realise what has happened here. People died to keep the left alive in Greece. And now we are back, after many obituaries and not a few self-inflicted wounds.' He added, with a wry pause, 'This is the beginning of something … We'll just have to see what that something is.' Giorgos's was not a cynical affectation. It was a prescient grasp upon the manifold conflicts the election of a government of the left would open up over the next six months.

Syriza, which stands for the Coalition of the Radical Left, was going to form a government. It was the first time in the history of Greece that such a force had won an election and formed an administration under its own name. 'Left' had a distinct meaning in Greece. It is one of those European countries in which the main political party of working-class people for much of the twentieth century was not a Labour-type, social democratic party – as in Britain or Germany – but a Communist Party or, in the case of Syriza, a development out of a once monolithic Communist tradition which had undergone a series of fractures. Left meant of the Communist heritage – that is of the historical tradition which was held by defenders of Western capitalism to be anti-democratic, and therefore rejected by free people in free elections. In any case, it was all meant to have been swept aside a generation ago, when the Berlin Wall came down. Communists had occasionally been in government elsewhere in Western Europe. But, with the exception of Cyprus, it had been as the much junior partner to larger social democratic parties – as in France in the early 1980s. The standard bearer of social democracy – Labour, to use the exceptionally British equivalent term – in Greece was Pasok. It had governed for most of the previous 35 years before crashing to 4.7 per cent on 25 January 2015 – a tenth of the vote it had been used to. That was one indication of the political earthquake which had hit this country of 11 million people, known fondly to most through hazily recalled ancient mythology or equally misty memories of fun holidays, great beaches and cheap drinks. The bitter realities of austerity-wracked Europe over the past decade have provided other images, refracted through a corporate-controlled media. They give some picture of the social disaster which has befallen the country.

As the disaster hit from 2008 onwards, images of suffering served largely as a pretext for blaming the victims. Just as, domestically, the right-wing tabloids in Britain scapegoat the poor, the ill and the marginalised, so they joined the elite chorus across Europe in demonising the people of a whole country. Greeks were lazy, had lied to get into the euro single currency, retired ridiculously early and spent their time sipping their drinks in the sun – all the while avoiding taxes and ripping off foreigners. The scale of tourism to Greece, one of its main earners, perversely provided some apparent evidence for the stereotype. The European elites projected that image of Greece through every media platform in the first half of 2015, as the new government tried to negotiate some relief within the European Union (EU) to crushing austerity. Every aspect of this image of the Greeks was a lie. Time is snatched through the demands and worries of work and monthly bills, which are common to the vast majority of people in the 28 countries of the EU, including Greece. But the experience millions of ordinary Europeans had of the country was of the relaxation, sunshine and the café culture they had enjoyed on their holidays. The more middle-brow 'cheating-Greeks' propaganda – which is what you get from the right-wing broadsheets and so much mainstream broadcasting – echoed two centuries of snobbery among the elites of Britain, Germany and France regarding southern Europe, and Greece in particular. In the grand tours of the European young aristocracy of the nineteenth century the adventurous would go as far as southern Italy. Only the hopelessly drunk or foolhardy would board a ship and head for the bandit lands of Greece. It was, in their imagination, rather eastern.

The identikit politicians of Europe dredged up that historical memory in response to Syriza's election victory. They held to an iron clad consensus that the way out of the deepest and most protracted economic crisis since the 1930s lay in cuts to welfare, slashing wages, rising unemployment and privatisation of remaining public assets. Greece, more than any other European country, had been the laboratory for those policies, bundled together under the dogma of austerity. In response, first came a wave of imaginative and combative movements against aspects of austerity – which included fanning the flames of racism – and the succession of governments which pursued them. Then, in a crescendo rising from 2012 to January 2015, opposition broke through at the ballot box with the election of a left committed to a radical escape from the austerity labyrinth.

The arrogant assertion by Europe's elites that there was no alternative to the policies they were forcing on reluctant voters at home was belied by the ferocity of their response to the democratic choice made by the Greek people. Syriza won the election with a slogan of hope for an alternative path, a break with the austerity years. Offering no alternative paths of their own, the elites' reaction in Greece and elsewhere was fear and hatred. Behind the anti-Greek stereotypes they fell back on lay an instinctive understanding that they faced a problem much greater than the rebellious behaviour of working people in the south-eastern tip of the continent. The insurgency in Greece was a leading edge of a broader, twin rejection across Europe of the old politics and politicians. It was a revolt against three decades of an economic orthodoxy that twisted the whole of society around the interests of a fabulously wealthy few. As the German chancellor Angela Merkel led the way in early summer in trying to force Syriza to capitulate, she faced a whiff of the kind of popular resistance which had shaken Greece. The Greek drama was at a crunch point, but the German press in May and June was dominated by coverage of continuous strikes by rail workers and other industrial action from schools to the post office and hospitals. Greece, in myriad ways, was providing an example. For the old political order it had to be extirpated, not simply argued against. That is why, early on in the Syriza-led government's clashes with the Troika of lenders – the International Monetary Fund (IMF), the European Central Bank (ECB), and the European Commission (EC) – the usual rules of diplomatic politesse went out the window. Germany's finance minister Wolfgang Schäuble repeatedly tried to humiliate the Greek representatives. The belligerence of the Troika fuelled the media's coverage. One unintended consequence was that interest in the fate of Greece's new government spread wider than the party-organised radical left seeking to emulate the example of the new Syriza government. Athens had potential allies. Not in official Europe, but among those suffering across the continent from the policies which Syriza was elected to end in Greece. A demonstration in March through Dublin against the Irish government introducing charges for water saw 80,000 people throng O'Connell Street. 'The main street in the capital was rammed with Greek flags,' an old friend and Irish MP, Richard Boyd Barrett, told me. 'The identification with Greece among ordinary Irish people is something I've never witnessed before.' Looking at the unfolding clash between Greece and the Troika, those wide layers of sympathisers with the Syriza government could find certain national particularities in developments in Greece. But they are specific features of a common experience.

Crisis of the old order

Greece has been the European country hardest hit by the global crisis unleashed following the financial crash of 2008. It is also the eurozone state – one of 19 which use the euro currency – upon which the most devastating austerity measures have been imposed by the Troika and successive Greek governments.

It is against that background that the Greek workers and social movements – popular campaigns, community struggles and the like – have sustained the highest levels of resistance to austerity and to an increasingly authoritarian state anywhere in Europe. Twentieth-century Greece had a turbulent history – two civil wars, six inter-state wars, occupation, dictatorship, coups and the overbearing role of the military in politics. That history is felt in the present. But Greece since the fall of the Colonels' Junta in 1974 proved to be remarkably stable – and modern. The Junta seized power in 1967. It was the only answer the monarchist right and its allies in the army had to the rising expectations of young people and to growing agitation by workers against the especially repressive and exploitative features of modern Greek capitalism and its state. Both of those were firmly anchored in the Western camp of the Cold War. The coup of 21 April 1967 could not halt the rising tide of the 1960s as it surged into one country after another on both sides of the Cold War divide. But it could, temporarily, dam it up. The result was that when the dictatorship fell in 1974 it was as if seven years of suspended development was suddenly unleashed in concentrated form. In a sense, 1968 came to Greece in 1974. When it did, it was as if the anti-Vietnam War movement, Woodstock and the wave of worker radicalisation in Western Europe all happened at the same time.

The old order was rocked back on its heels and it was forced to adapt. The period following 1974 – the years of the *metapolitefsi*, or regime change – saw the creation of a new political settlement, with new political parties. The previous set up comprised a party of the left (a legal front for the banned Communist Party), a liberal, but anti-communist, pro-business party, and a right-wing, monarchist and militarist party. That political arrangement had failed in the 1960s to contain the left as a political force (the United Democratic Left shocked the Greek business class and generals by doing unexpectedly well in the general election of 1958) or to curb rising militancy by working people, students and young people, which burst onto the streets in July 1965. Hence the coup two years later. The new, post-coup arrangement required new parties. It also depended on a social compact. That meant the business class perforce granting concessions to workplace militancy and demands for welfare provision. The next four decades saw uninterrupted rule by the centre left and centre right, Pasok and New Democracy. We shall turn to them shortly, but for now the important point is that the political order which came crashing down in 2015 was not an aberrant hangover from Greek history. It was the very modern, very European, essentially two-party system of alternating rule between centre left and centre right, with both committed in the last 20 years to broadly the same policies.

The 1990s demonstrated the modernity of Greece, not its supposed Balkan mentality. While Balkan wars engulfed neighbouring Yugoslavia that decade, Greece smoothly joined the twenty-first-century project of the euro. It seemed, by the beginning of our century, that old Europe was ineluctably modernising – the south becoming more like the centrist, post-ideological north. In the person of Costas Simitis, Greece had had its own Blairite photocopy as prime minister between 1996 and 2004. Many of the politicians and commentators who claim now that the economic and social disaster in Greece is a result of its failure to modernise are the same people who, only a little over a decade ago, as the Athens Olympics took place, were hailing the success of the modernising prime ministerships of Pasok's Simitis and New Democracy's Constantinos Mitsotakis. Between them Pasok and New Democracy, with some smaller forces, implemented the shock therapy of austerity from 2009 to 2015. What the election results in January 2015 revealed was a popular backlash against the austerity parties on such a scale that it redrew the political map.

The ruins of the centre left

Most dramatic was the fate of Pasok. When party founder Andreas Papandreou closed his victorious election campaign in 1981 he spoke to a rally of nearly 1 million people (rather disturbingly, for anyone of the left, to the Teutonic foot-stomping of Carl Orff's 'Carmina Burana'). In January 2015, Pasok limped over the 3 per cent threshold for representation in the parliament. Andreas Papandreou was from one of the great dynasties which dominated Greek politics during the last century and which were as important as ideology in the formation of governing alliances and political parties. His son, George, became prime minister in 2009 and signed up to the Troika's memorandum, which began the austerity programme. Pasok, under a new leader, collapsed to third place in the 2012 elections. George Papandreou left to found his own party – the Movement of Democratic Socialists. It failed to get over the 3 per cent threshold. When Andreas broke from the liberal centre in the 1970s to form Pasok, he could claim justification in splitting the centre bloc against the monarchist right because he was giving a genuine voice to the social democratic left, independent from the liberals. It is a mark of the degeneration of the centre left that his son tried to provide a voice only for the Papandreous. And it was not to be heard beyond their own parlour. Complacent social democratic leaders elsewhere should take note. One outgrowth of the crisis of Pasok was the proliferation of other centre-left parties attempting to occupy its space. The old saw about the radical, socialist left – that it is forever split into micro, rival groups – applies to today's centre left in Greece. One formation which did make it into the parliament was To Potami (The River). It had been created overnight in 2014 to fight the European Parliament elections. Very much a media confection, it is the creation of TV presenter Stavros Theodorakis (no relation to the famous left-wing composer Mikis). In so doing, Theodorakis was merely following a venerable tradition – in Greece and elsewhere – of charismatic figures founding their own political vehicles. But whereas the Papandreou and Karamanlis clans could draw on great reserves of social capital in launching their political projects (Pasok and New Democracy) in the 1970s, The River is somewhat shallow.

Theodorakis made his name with a TV show called *The Protagonists*. It took up sympathetically the stories of the 'marginalised' – prisoners, Roma and so on. Nothing wrong with that, especially given the harsh social policies of every Greek government in the crisis years. But for Theodorakis these scandals were aberrations from the civilised European norm. So the political logic was already clear before he launched the party. Greece needed more moderating influence from Brussels, Berlin and Paris to trim the old national-traditionalists, of left and right, who revelled in chauvinism rather than euro-cosmopolitanism. His message was amplified within the echo chamber of the European media, who largely shared with their fellow TV presenter an outlook of modernising liberalism.

The problem – as Theodorakis found out – is that scapegoating Muslims, persecuting Roma, suspending human rights provisions, and bullying opponents are not the preserve of the benighted Balkans. They are the policy, programme and political reflex of the whole of the European establishment in the crisis years.

In the course of the election campaign the pro-business thrust of Theodorakis's centrism became more apparent. The truth is that there is no such thing as a centre which preserves pristine equidistance between the poles of left and right. The centre has beliefs. The Liberal Democrats in Britain showed theirs by staying in coalition with the most vicious of Tory governments for five years solid. The TV presenter is against the left on the whole. He refused to join the social democratic left in the European Parliament. Some confused commentators imputed a principled and radical stance to that decision: that he was against all the old crooks. In reality, he wants nothing whatsoever to do with the left. He made that clear as Syriza took office and faced the wrath of the Troika. To Potami sought to undermine the government and force the creation of a national unity coalition which would be committed to the austerity regime the voters had rejected. One example serves to show the depths of To Potami's commitment to big business and the thinness of its claim to be a champion of human rights. The Syriza-led government tabled measures to liberalise Greece's inhuman prison conditions in April. On television, Theodorakis is the supposed champion of the rights of the marginalised – including prisoners – yet his party voted against the provisions. In the following months his anti-leftism became even more pronounced. The liberal Theodorakis took up the themes of the old authoritarian right.

The three-headed centre right

Across Western Europe the decades of post-war stability allowed for a channelling of politics from the mass, violent clashes of the 1930s into the more pacific conduits of parliamentary democracy. Christian Democracy emerged – or, rather, was crafted with great resource and effort – as a broad church for a range of right and centre-right forces which had, in the interwar years, fought for political power under their own banners: national conservatives, industrialists, religious conservatives, liberals, fascists … right-wing chancers of all kinds.

In Greece the process was delayed and took a peculiar course. That was due to the anti-Communist civil war of 1945–9 and the entrenching in power – backed by the US and Britain – of a monarchist, authoritarian right for whom political violence was customary. There could be no return for the Greek capitalist class to monarcho-military methods after the fall of the Junta in 1974. A referendum held in that year abolished the monarchy. Instead, they cohered around the patrician figure of Constantine Karamanlis, who had remained outside Greece during the coup years and returned to found the New Democracy party. Italian Christian Democracy had had the luxury of 20 years to meld together competing right-wing forces (bound together by golden threads of corruption of Croesus proportions, the mafia and the immense social resources of the Catholic Church). New Democracy had to do it all in the course of the tempestuous mid 1970s.

One consequence was that New Democracy was dominated by old-style paternalistic politicians of the right. The familial and institutional connections with the traditionally anti-democratic establishment remained strong.

At the same time, like the rest of the centre right in the 1980s and 1990s, it tried to be the party of economic liberalism – in the Thatcher-Reagan model. In popular appeal, however, national conservative themes of patriotism, religious Orthodoxy, anti-Communism and anti-immigrant racism played heavily.

These tensions within New Democracy burst out in 2010 when George Papandreou signed up to the first austerity memorandum. New Democracy leader Antonis Samaras came from the national chauvinist,[6] populist wing of the party. He led New Democracy in parliament to vote against the memorandum, on the narrowest of party motives. That prompted ideologically committed neoliberals, led by Dora Bakoyanni, to split, temporarily. Bakoyanni is the standard bearer of the free market, modernising right – and also scion of New Democracy's Mitsotakis clan. The third wing of the party is the old patrician Karamanlis camarilla. Today Bakoyanni is back with New Democracy. But her tendency is not in command of the party.

Leadership stayed in the hands of Samaras, despite his defeat at the hands of Syriza, until he was forced to step down in July 2015. The chasm between the Bakoyanni and Samaras wings remained. It is more than ideological. Samaras led a right-wing nationalist split from New Democracy in the 1990s. He returned just in time to be given the leadership in 2009 over the head of Bakoyanni and the Mitsotakis clan, who had remained loyal to the party all those years.

The argument between them back in 2010 over the first memorandum is instructive. Bakoyanni denounced Samaras's opportunism in not voting – as every other centre-right party in Europe did in similar circumstances – for the pro-business austerity package. His reply was that he was not simply trying to ensure that rival Pasok bore the brunt for the popular backlash that was to come. He also tellingly said that if New Democracy did not voice opposition, then the only people opposing the memorandum would be Syriza, the Communists and the left, and that that would be a recipe for disaster. Bakoyanni answered that at some point New Democracy would have to embrace the memorandum policy anyway, so all that delaying would do would be to legitimise the idea that there was any alternative to austerity. In 2012 New Democracy did indeed make a sharp turn to voting for new austerity measures in parliament. It was this decision that prompted a split by Panos Kammenos and a group of MPs from New Democracy to form the Independent Greeks, ANEL. It got back into parliament in 2012 and again in 2015. ANEL's character – anti-memorandum yet also national chauvinist and xenophobic

– and its emergence can be understood only in the context of the decision taken by the party of Greek big business, early on in the crisis, to oppose the austerity memorandums. Samaras could claim that by refusing to endorse austerity for two years he had bought New Democracy a longer lease of life. Certainly, Pasok's collapse proved much more severe. But Samaras's gambit came at great price. It did not stop the left becoming the main expression of the anti-austerity backlash. And it deepened the schisms inside the right. There was the emergence of ANEL. There was also the success of the neo-Nazi Golden Dawn, which entered the parliament in 2012 and came third in January 2015.

The reconfiguring of the right in Greece is, in hothouse microcosm, part of a Europe-wide phenomenon. The singular pole of Christian Democracy is fragmenting, allowing a variety of right-wing forces – from anti-European nationalists to outright fascists – to re-emerge in their own party formations.

The Front National in France, dismissed as a short-lived Poujadist protest movement in 1983, is the largest iceberg to calve from the retreating glacier. The most successful ruling-class party in history – the British Tory party – now faces serious competition from Ukip. Even Germany, beneficiary of the euro arrangement, has the right-wing, populist Alternative für Deutschland above the 5 per cent threshold for election to parliament.

The first right-wing break from New Democracy had been LAOS, a racist-nationalist party which entered the parliament in 2007. Its leadership contained veteran fascists. It joined a pro-memorandum caretaker coalition in 2011, and suffered at the subsequent general election a few months later as a result. Out of its collapse arose the outright fascists of Golden Dawn. Some LAOS MPs also defected back to New Democracy. That did not mark the restoration of the 'moderate' centre right. It served to accelerate New Democracy's turn to authoritarianism and racism. Both became central as it governed, with coalition support from Pasok and Dimar, a pro-market breakaway from Syriza, between 2012 and 2015. There is an affinity between Makis Voridis – former LAOS now New Democracy MP – and Samaras. Voridis was a notorious fascist storm-trooper while a student. There is a well-known picture of him from that time wielding an axe on the hunt for left-wing students.

Samaras may not have personally wielded an axe. But his entire political line has been to reach deep into the collective memory of the right, digging up every anti-Communist smear and innuendo of the civil war years. The confection is spiced with virulent anti-immigrant, anti-Muslim racism.

Samaras began the election campaign in January 2015 in earnest by visiting the far-flung border between Greece and Turkey marked by the river Evros. It is here that border control has been handed willingly to European corporation Frontex, paid handsomely to keep migrants out. There is, in effect, a premium for every black or brown person who washes up on the banks of the river – lifeless.

[Samaras made the crudest of anti-immigrant pitches in an attempt to deflect popular resistance to austerity. He went further than even Marine Le Pen, leader of the Front National, in the wake of the *Charlie Hebdo* atrocity in Paris, which took place during the Greek general election campaign. He said it was the result of mass migration into Europe. But the classic playing of the race-card at that election was not enough to keep him in power.]

The new government

There was celebration, but not euphoria, as Alexis Tsipras sat down to form a government following the election triumph. Indeed, the election campaign had been characterised by what we might call a 'tempered excitement'. One reason was that it took place in winter. Greece in January might have had al fresco weather by London standards, but it was far from conducive to a vibrant street campaign of rallies and public events. A second reason was that, with two weeks to go before election day, it seemed settled that Syriza would win, the only question was by how much. Samaras tried, at the last minute, to modify his racist, anti-Communist campaign by attempting to present himself as a one-nation figure, promising that there would be no further attacks on pensions. It was not credible. The weekend before the vote, the newspaper *Ta Nea*, a kind of institution of the centre left, in effect conceded that Syriza would form the next government. It began the shift in line which was later embraced by the European establishment. A Syriza government was going to be a reality. The aim would have to be to moderate it, to drain it of energy, and to transform it one way or another into a variant of the old politics which voters – working-class voters especially – had decisively rejected. But the biggest reason the atmosphere was less celebratory than in 2009, when George Papandreou won the election at the start of the crisis, was the sentiment among the mass of Greeks who had suffered in the intervening six years. It was not cynical. They were voting, after all, for a party whose message was hope and change. But there was a degree of scepticism. That was founded on the experiences they had been through in seeing one government after another fail to arrest the catastrophic social collapse. And it arose from the fact that millions of ordinary Greeks had taken politics into their own hands in a series of intense battles against austerity. That social resistance, unmatched anywhere else in Europe, might not have succeeded in halting the formal passing by parliament of the austerity policies demanded under the memorandums negotiated with the Troika of Greece's creditors. But it had maintained and developed a level of popular organisation. It had blunted and slowed the pace of attack. And it had brought down one government after another. People hoped to hope that the new government would be different. But it was not that desperate hope which comes paradoxically from abject despair. There was both a widespread understanding of the scale of the crisis facing the incoming government and, consequently, the realisation among the networks of trade unionists, social movement campaigners, and activists of the left – notably in the base of Syriza – that the period of intense mobilisation had not ended with the election victory. Rather, there would be fresh battles to come. Despite the enormous suffering, the morale of working-class Greece was not broken. Had it been, then the right's message would have had a far greater resonance. The old political system, which had served the Greek oligarchs so well, was, however, broken.

It had been pulled apart along two axes – left and right, and pro- and anti-memorandum. The whole of the left – Syriza, the Communist Party and the Antarsya anti-capitalist coalition – advanced at the election of 2015 compared with June 2012. On the right, it was those parties which, however speciously, proclaimed themselves to be opposed to the austerity memorandums which held their ground. ANEL ended up with 13 MPs. The fascist Golden Dawn came third with 17. Golden Dawn's vote was marginally down on 2012, but significantly less than the 9.4 per cent it had polled in the European Parliament elections in 2014. The resilience of the fascists' vote was alarming. It had not been crushed by the wave of anti-fascist campaigning, peaking in the months following the murder by Golden Dawn of popular anti-racist rapper, Pavlos Fyssas, in September 2013. But the movement was not without impact. It had forced into the mainstream the demand to isolate the fascists. That was a battle which was to continue throughout 2015 as the fascists sought to position themselves to take advantage of any halting or stumbling by the new government in its protracted negotiations with the Troika to lift the austerity regime on Greece. It had also succeeded in checking the fascists' advance. The detail beneath the raw voting figures revealed an important shift in the base of support for Golden Dawn. Previously, it had polled well among the demographic groups where the left had tended to do best. It was a competitor for young, angry and unemployed men. (Its support among women of all demographic groups was markedly less.)

In 2015, however, it lost support heavily among those groups and in inner city areas. It offset those loses with increased support in rural areas and among the older strata who were the bedrock for New Democracy. In other words, and within certain limits, Golden Dawn emerged from the elections in third place, but as more of a traditional party of the right with less of a claim to be an insurgent, anti-system party.[7] It was not where it wanted to be. It sought to recover strategically by positioning itself in the new parliament as an anti-memorandum force – therefore utterly opposed to the old parties, including New Democracy, and dishonestly on the side of the government in so far as it challenged the foreign lenders. The battle against Golden Dawn, and to prevent it from being able to rehabilitate itself in this way, therefore remained critical. The space the fascists sought to exploit resulted in part from the composition of the coalition government Tsipras formed in order to secure a parliamentary majority.

The day after the election he announced that Syriza would be forming a government with the national chauvinist, but anti-memorandum, ANEL as junior coalition partners. Together, the parties had a working majority of 162 MPs out of 300. There was, understandably, great confusion on the international left, which had been ecstatic at the Syriza victory. There was also concern among many Syriza activists and voters. 'This is a terrible decision,' Thanos, an LGBT activist in Athens told me:

> I marched with the Syriza youth on the Pride demonstration last year and voted for the party. Now it has gone into government with a party of bigots. One of the ANEL MPs was condemned throughout the continent because of his homophobic abuse about the prime minister of Luxembourg being gay. I was overjoyed last night. This coalition decision really hurts.

An indication of the decision had come the night before in Tsipras's victory speech. He had emphasised national unity in the coming battle with the Troika to end austerity. He spoke of a government of social salvation. He did not speak of a victory of the left, even though that is what had happened. The public rationale for the coalition was that Syriza had no choice. It would not, could not, go into coalition with the parties of the centre left, who had made it clear that the condition would be the repudiation of the anti-memorandum stance on which Syriza had won the election. The Communist Party had 13 MPs, but refused to enter any coalition. That just left ANEL as an anti-memorandum party. The reassurance to the left in such an arrangement was that ANEL would be very much a junior partner and that the government would implement left-wing policies, including over ending the persecution of migrants – despite ANEL's objections. We explore later to what extent that turned out to be the case in the course of the government's first six months.

The actual thinking behind the decision was not some ad hoc response to just falling short of an outright majority. It pointed to an underlying strategic approach. First, there was the alternative of forming a minority government. There is little point in rehearsing the arguments around that here given the actual turn of events. One aspect is worth mentioning, however. There would naturally be difficulties in governing with two seats short of a majority, though the fragmentation of the parliamentary opposition meant it would be even more difficult for it to combine together on any single vote to defeat the government. Be that as it may, one reaction to Syriza's predicament from friends abroad who, rightly, placed great hope in the Greek election result and did not want to see Syriza's efforts swallowed in cynical denunciations, was to proclaim that it was constitutionally impossible to have a minority government in Greece. As news spread of the coalition deal, I remember hearing from parts of the radical left across Europe that there was no legal alternative. That was not true, as a glance at the unambiguous Greek constitution would show.

In their effort to shield the left's election victory in Greece from the kind of carping criticism which is forever ready to shout treachery –

a destructive Pavlovian reaction which destroys hope and on which nothing of value is built – some on the left were abandoning their own critical faculties. I recall the moment now not because it was of great importance in its own right. Instead, the debate about the formation of the coalition was but an early example of a series of legitimate arguments, which are developed in this book, about the choices and strategies the left should adopt – particularly at key moments of decision, when there is a fork in the path. When conducted from the standpoint of solidarity with the mass of the Greek people, Syriza and the Greek left against austerity, those arguments are about strengthening the Europe-wide movement against the same things they are resisting. Evading them would turn out, as the Syriza government bedded in, to undermine that process.

The second difficult truth about the coalition deal was that it was not struck in the heat of the moment. For months the leadership of Syriza around Tsipras had indicated that it would favour such a coalition. The reasoning was that Greece faced a national emergency. The Troika was behaving like the financial equivalent of Hitler's devastating occupation of the country in the Second World War. Even with 42 per cent of the vote,[8] the left could not hope to meet such an emergency nor to govern without finding allies. So talks with ANEL were under way well before the polls closed. That is why the meeting between Tsipras and Kammenos to agree the coalition deal was over and done with so quickly. Recalling this is not to recite some atrocity story. The Syriza leadership had a clear strategy and honest arguments supporting it, the ones sketched out here and explored later. By succeeding against the odds in winning the election, Syriza, a party of the radical left, was in a position to implement that strategy and, therefore, to bring to life historic debates about how the left could take power; how to win permanent and fundamental change in favour of working people, and a host of other questions which had animated the left internationally for a century.

In telling the story of Syriza's rise and its first six months in office, this book seeks to highlight those political debates, which are now, thanks to the breakthrough in January, of interest to a wider audience than just the traditional left. So I have tried to avoid traditional left language, which may not be understood by that audience. I do so in the spirit of solidarity with the left in Greece, a country I have known well for over 30 years, and from the standpoint of trying to contribute to the development of movements for social transformation and of a powerful radical left across Europe.

In foregrounding points of debate and criticism there is always a danger of sowing demoralisation and cynicism. Those are breeding grounds for the right. It thrives on the resigned common sense that nothing can ever change fundamentally. The great socialist writer Paul Foot once said, 'How can a socialist possibly be a cynic? Scepticism, yes. Question everything was Karl Marx's motto. But cynicism, never.' There are at least two ways to demoralise a hopeful movement for change. There is outright cynicism, often masquerading as world-weary wisdom. Ask anyone who knows about ancient Greek philosophy and they will tell you that Diogenes the Cynic was not a very popular man. But the other is the path of Dr Peter Pangloss, the character in Voltaire's *Candide*. His standard refrain was to say that all is for the best in this best of all possible worlds. Evading the difficult questions posed by the left being in government in Greece does not do justice to the new generation of young people across Europe who, more than anyone else, have been the victims of the austerity disaster. For the truly radical development in Greece – and in the Spanish state and elsewhere – over the last few years is not that people have struggled and then elected better politicians with the old, conventional under-standing that it is through them that real change comes. It is that we have seen a glimpse of a new way entirely of doing things, one where ordinary people begin to formulate their own answers and own ways of organising. They have created not just protest movements, but have pointed to how we may organise in new ways our lives, the economy and society as a whole: a politics of participation, not merely of representation by politicians with more left-wing policies.

The possibility of such a radical break from the old is a central theme of this book. It is also an echo of the last period of great hope for progressive change in Greece, Europe and beyond. That is, the upsurge of the 1960s, which arrived late, but all the more energetically, in Greece a few years later. I first went to Greece in 1983 and met an activist on what seemed to be another planet of the large, variegated, Greek radical and revolutionary left. Dina was a little older than me and had come into the movement in 1979, joining one of the several big Maoist organisations, which were on the brink of implosion. Already, by Easter 1983, there was a feeling that Thatcher and Reagan were ascendant and that the tide was ebbing from the great upsurges of 10 years earlier. So I asked her what it was like coming into the movement at the end of that tumultuous decade. 'My dear,' she said, 'It was like arriving late at a party. You know – you climb up the stairs to the hosts' flat. Everyone is tumbling down the stairs. And they are telling you just how good it had been.' We stayed in touch. Still on the left, she messaged me as the results came in on election night and Syriza's victory became assured. 'You remember that party?' she said, 'I think the music just got going again.'

January takes its name from Janus, the Roman god of doorways, beginnings and ends, transitions. The election marked the beginning of a period of transition – 'Between things ended and things begun', as nineteenth-century American poet Walt Whitman put it. To see how and why that transition played out so dramatically over just a few succeeding months, it is necessary to understand first of all the nature of Syriza as a party and how it came to office.

CHAPTER TWO

The Resisted Rise of Syriza

Syriza was formed in 2004 and just scraped over the threshold to enter parliament in elections that year. Eleven years later, it was in government and the dominant party in Greek politics. Its rise as a governing party is inseparable from the profound political crises in Greece throughout those 11 years and from the social polarisation and resistance to an economic catastrophe of 1930s proportions. That political crisis and succession of massive popular mobilisations were not simply raw materials to be worked upon by leaders of the radical left to sculpt a victory at the polls in 2015. They comprised the actions and political choices of millions of people, concentrated at key moments in the crisis, and also the collapse of various strategies by the traditional parties of government to weather the storm. So, in telling the story of the rise of Syriza, this and the following chapters will first look at the overall course of the party's growth and its relationship to those fundamental developments. Then they will consider the popular resistance and the hollowing out of the old, *ancien regime*.

From 1991 to 2009: the inbetweener

The driving force in the creation of Syriza was another party called Synaspismos. It emerged from a split in the Greek Communist Party in 1991. Both sides were weakened in the split, especially with the loss to both of the party's youth section, KNE, which went off to form its own organisation, NAR, the New Left Current. The orthodox[9] Communist Party, the KKE, through a combination of fabled discipline and steering left based on an ideology and verbal radicalism which could hold some attraction for militant young people, was able in the course of the 1990s to rebuild its student and youth presence and avoid fading away. Synaspismos fared worse. Few could imagine that its youth leader at the Athens Polytechnic, Alexis Tsipras, was a future prime minister when they saw him sat, somewhat lonely, behind a campaign stall in those years. It was there, in fact, that I met him in the mid 1990s at a youth anti-war event. Tsipras had been in KNE and was prominent in the militant high school occupations of 1990–1, negotiating for the movement with the government. He had unfashionably gone with Synaspismos at the time of the split.

Synaspismos in the 1990s had something of an 'inbetweener' problem. In profile and in self-identity the party, which hovered a little over the 3 per cent threshold for parliamentary representation, sat between Pasok and the KKE. Ideologically, it lacked the popularly understood traditions of both. Pasok had the legacy of Papandreou and his mythologised achievements in office in his first term. The KKE had the inheritance of the liberation struggle, civil war and decades of sacrifice under illegality of its members. In their different ways that gave both a coherent placing in the voters' minds, occupying the positions of traditional Greek left and of moderate social democracy. Politically, Synaspismos was caught between, whether it was an outrider of social democratic Pasok, looking to form a coalition with it or an insurgent anti-establishment party. If the latter, what was its strategy given that it was dwarfed by Pasok and consistently smaller in membership, activists and votes than the KKE? What it could provide, however, was a more creative intellectual space than the dogmatic KKE or the eclectic, anti-intellectual machine politics of Pasok. It had the intellectual inheritance of the Eurocommunist wing of the left. That strand, emerging out of the Western European Communist parties, had taken seriously the implications of the official turn by the Soviet Union in the late 1950s to a doctrine of decades of peaceful coexistence with the capitalist West. It had also been more porous to the 'new social movements', often anti-authority, of 1968, and to engagement with thinkers who saw in them novel strategies for a period of diverse social struggles as opposed to the clash of forces, and of East and West, in the class struggle. That brought a great diversity of ideas and political orientations within the party. One indication of that is that, as Costas Simitis began what turned out to be eight years in office as Pasok's version to Tony Blair in 1996, some of Synaspismos proved susceptible to the kind of 'Third Way' modernising ideology promoted by Blairite thinkers, such as Anthony Giddens. When Simitis spoke as a guest at the 1996 Synaspismos conference, around half the delegates gave him a standing ovation. What was to transform that into the party which came to power in 2015 on a programme of real, left-wing reforms, not a Blairite liquidation of old socialist policies?

It was the eruption of the twin international movements against the excesses of corporate capitalism and against the Iraq war between 1999 and 2003 which pulled Synaspismos in a more radical direction. They, too, pushed its leadership to form the Syriza electoral coalition, incorporating a range of smaller forces largely to Synaspismos's left. Synaspismos was not the only, nor the first, organised force on the Greek left to make a turn to embracing the new movements. But it was the only one which already had some purchase in the official political scene – that is, in the parliament and electoral arena. In that, it resembled the Italian party of refounded communism, Rifondazione. It was also able to rejuvenate itself and to become an electoral expression of the common sense in those anti-war and anti-capitalist (or *altermondialiste*) movements. That common sense was for some combination of parliamentary representation and pressure from a mass movement to bring about radical reform. It was not the left of Synaspismos, but its centrist leadership under Nikos Konstantopoulos[10] who embarked on refreshing the tired party through launching Syriza as, at first, a limited electoral coalition.

With 3.3 per cent the new Syriza coalition succeeded, just, in the 2004 general election, in maintaining a parliamentary presence. New Democracy won the election and formed a government lasting five years. With Pasok in opposition, the perennial strategic problem for Synaspismos/Syriza re-emerged: whether to position itself as a potential coalition partner with Pasok at the next elections and, if not, what was the alternative?

At the conference that year the left won a majority and Alekos Alavanos became leader, prevailing against those who had wanted to dump the radical elements in the Syriza coalition straight after they had served to push the party over the 3 per cent threshold at the election. Then the decision in 2006 by Rifondazione to go into government with the centre left produced a further rebuke to those who looked to doing the same in Greece. The Italian experience proved a disaster. Rifondazione in parliament ended up voting for the deployment of Italian troops to Afghanistan, even though it was through the anti-war movement that the party had grown. So great was the backlash in Italy among voters that the resulting collapse of Rifondazione at the polls warned off even the most moderate elements in Synaspismos from advocating a similar course. The impact across Europe was to encourage among many young activists the other common sense of the early 2000s, and which persists to this day: that any discussion of overall strategy with a view to pulling together a political force to challenge the old parties would end up emulating them; the only true radicalism was for the movements of social protest to be autonomous from politics, parties and corrupting general strategies.

In 2006 into 2007 in Greece, there was a huge wave of occupations by university students. It succeeded in stopping the government changing the constitution to introduce private, for-profit universities. It claimed the scalp of the education minister. The movement sought not to evade politics and its central decision-making in the state, but to confront it. 'We are doing the politics which Pasok refuses to do,' I heard a student radical of the anti-capitalist left tell an occupation meeting that winter:

Those here who say we should be decentralised have to ask themselves this: 'Is the government in trouble because hundreds of occupations are happening with their own separate demands and actions; or because we have created a national coordinating body?'

The extent and politicisation of the student movement meant it was a point of discussion in every working-class and middle-class family with a relative at university. Its victory answered one question, but posed another. Collective struggle could defeat a government's policy and force out one of its hard-nosed ministers. But what would be the replacement? In the autumn of 2008 came the start of the global financial crisis leading to the Great Recession and the imposition of austerity policies in Greece, leading to an economic collapse on the scale depicted in John Steinbeck's novels of the US in the 1930s.

Syriza had won 5 per cent of the vote in nationwide elections in 2007 and drew into its coalition some more organisations of the radical left. The support offered the student occupations in parliament by Alavanos in combative attacks on the government helped it attract youth support. Though the government was tired and already looked on its way out, Pasok in parliament and in the composition of its leadership was flatfooted, still damaged in the eyes of its historic base by the Simitis modernising years. It was similar to the British Labour Party at the time, as Blair and Gordon Brown in this period lost millions of voters. Pasok, too, appeared exhausted. For a brief period Syriza stood at around 16 per cent in the polls as it attracted many disaffected Pasok voters. But the habits of the two-party system did not die so easily. There had yet to be crisis events of sufficient depth to rupture habitual and traditional political allegiances. So, as New Democracy presided over the first gales of recession in 2008 into 2009, there was a swing back to Pasok. The first social eruption came in December of that year with the youth revolt (see the following chapter). By then, Alavanos had made way as leader for the much younger Tsipras. He had attracted a significant youth following when he stood as a candidate in the election for the mayor of Athens in 2006. Against powerful moderate elements in Synaspismos, Tsipras – and Alavanos in parliament, where he still led the group of MPs – refused to join the hang 'em and flog 'em condemnation of the December youth riots. That stance, combined with the, albeit temporary, earlier spike in the polls, strengthened the forces inside Synaspismos, in alliance with radical elements in the wider Syriza coalition, who rejected the idea of fighting the election due in 2009 as an appendage of Pasok.

From 2009 to 2012: breakdown and breakthrough

The worsening economic situation throughout 2009 was but a whiff of what was to come. It was bad. But it seemed little different from previous contractions. That was what all the politicians said. It was with that expectation in voters' minds that there was a return of much of its traditional support to Pasok. George Papandreou won the election in October with 45 per cent. Syriza secured around 4 per cent, once again behind the Communist Party, KKE. Few saw portents of the extraordinary upheavals of the next three years. The Synaspismos party conference maintained support for the wider Syriza formation. But it also slipped back towards being a kind of ginger group relation to Pasok. The emphasis was on parliamentary tactics aimed at trying to influence the larger party rather than on a hard political fight to replace it as the main pole of politics among the working class, young people and progressives. In the rifts that opened up, Alavanos and the more radical components of the Syriza coalition argued for a militant policy of support for the – by then – emergent strikes and social resistance to the government. But it was only later that he argued for breaking with the economic constraints of the euro single currency and membership of the EU. If necessary, that meant Greece leaving both.

By the spring of 2010 the scale of the economic disaster was obvious. Papandreou moved to sign the first of the austerity memorandums with the Troika of lenders. The social devastation that caused and the reasons why successive Greek governments imposed austerity are explored in the next two chapters. A general strike and nationwide protest demonstrations held on 5 May were gigantic. Half a million people took to the streets of Athens.

We will turn to consider in more detail the movements against austerity of which the May demonstrations marked the start. In looking now, from the point of view of their impact on Syriza's rise first to eclipse Pasok and then to form a government, it is necessary to repeat that the movements had a life, potential and effect of their own. They were not simply, as the kind of routine thinking which had failed to anticipate such developments maintains, a means to stir people up and then corral them behind an electoral force to do the real job of bringing about change. That had been the view of Pasok over the years when, as in 2009, it had rhetorically supported popular protests against the right wing in government with a singular strategy of winning votes to hoist it back into office.

The mass strikes and confrontations of May 2010 vindicated all those on the radical left who rejected fashionable notions that the Greek working class, whose trade unions were led largely by supporters of Pasok, had changed fundamentally, was bureaucratised, and was no longer capable of the kinds of struggles it had waged in the heady days of the 1970s and 1980s. Given the scale of struggle seen from the vantage point of 2015 – 34 one-day (occasionally two-day) general strikes, some 800 sectional strikes and many more labour confrontations since 2010, it is difficult to imagine that anyone could have held that view back then. But they did. And it was one immediate casualty of a wave of militant struggle not seen since the 1970s. A second was Syriza itself. A grouping of four MPs led by Fotis Kouvelis split from the party in June 2010. It went on to move in a pro-austerity direction. Kouvelis and his grouping, which adopted the name Dimar – the Democratic Left – had long since identified as modernisers and had an affinity with the Simitis stable. They shared the belief that the free market – with some modest social tempering – and European integration would bring greater social freedom. The illiberal features of Greece, in this thinking, were as much the fault of a Jurassic left as they were of the conservative right. For the left-liberal modernisers the central problem was what Blair called 'the forces of conservatism', under which he labelled not merely old-style Tories, but all the institutions of the working-class movement.

Second, the mobilisations of traditionally Pasok-supporting trade unionists and others against Papandreou's imposition of austerity deepened the long-term rift between the party and its voters. That also led a range of Pasok politicians to break from the party in an effort to save themselves from defeat at one election or another. That, in turn, had a contradictory impact on Syriza. On the one hand, it opened space to win over masses of working people, whose break with Pasok was much more decisive than two years earlier. But it also created a pressure to come to some old-style, party-machine arrangement with career politicians, who only yesterday had been happy to support austerity measures and to denounce the left. Today – without any change in themselves, but with a transforming political landscape – they were jumping ship and relaunching their careers.

It was not just some remaining elements within Synaspismos whose thinking was, like Dimar's, closer to Pasok's than to a fundamentally radical alternative which led it to promote a series of such social democratic defectors. Doing so also seemed impeccably good tactics, according to the seasoned political wisdom of the apparatuses of the parliamentary parties of the left and centre left. Just as $1 + 1 = 2$, so surely ex-Pasok figures would add their personal following to Syriza's rising share of the vote. That common sense was refuted at regional elections in October 2010.

Alavanos and a grouping of left forces in Syriza argued against the strategy of the Synaspismos majority and for a more radical electoral platform. So deep was the division that Syriza was split in the election for the Attiki region, which includes Athens and is the most populous in Greece. Alavanos stood as an independent and won 2.2 per cent. The recently departed Dimar took 3.8 per cent; the official Syriza candidate, 6.3 per cent. Doubtless the division cost them all votes. But even so, the ex-Pasok candidate who ran for Syriza did far worse than predicted, and far worse than the defunct equations of political reckoning had led people to expect. What was happening was deeper than people rejecting policies or expressing a protest vote. It was the beginnings of a sundering of trust between the popular masses and the old political monoliths and personnel. People were saying no to the old politicians as much as they were to their unpopular policies. The success of the small anti-capitalist coalition, Antarsya, in getting councillors elected in several cities in those local elections underscored the point. It was to be proven most dramatically as Syriza in the next 18 months renewed its commitment to a radical course. Its success on that path proved at least one thing: newer faces were exactly what people wanted.

There was a backlash inside Synaspismos against the strategy of subordinating a radical message to the failed electoral tactic of providing a landing pad for unreconstructed social democrats on the rat-run from a sinking ship. Without belittling the fight conducted by the left within Syriza and Synaspismos, the main factor in steering the party and coalition leftwards in 2011 was the still greater level of popular struggle as the austerity policies of the first memorandum tipped the Greek economy over the cliff.

The Egyptian revolution in January, with its tactic of occupying Tahrir Square and other public spaces, inspired the 'movement of the squares' in first the Spanish state, and then Greece in May and June. This new form of resistance, alongside but initially at odds with ongoing strikes and more traditional modes of popular struggle, gave rise to fresh political debates and possibilities. They are considered in the next chapter. Viewed from the angle of Syriza's development and growth, the party's younger activists in particular were heavily involved in the squares movement alongside the anti-capitalist left outside of the party. Both lacked the double inhibition of the Communist Party that the squares movement was both not under its

δεν πληρώνουμε
δεν χρωσαμε ⑦

leadership and also new-fangled – its form and contradictory currents taken as evidence that it was the expression of class forces alien to a mummified conception of what the genuine proletariat and its struggles looked like. For the KKE there was a circular logic to this justification of circling the wagons and keeping its militants out of the squares. The proof of a true working-class and socialist movement was to be found in the extent to which it was drawn to and led by the true party of the working class – the Communist Party. That the squares movement was not thus led was evidence of it not being progressive. It would be a mistake to give a radical gloss to such a movement by swelling its numbers and participating. Thus the KKE's abstention from that and other movements became the justification for the policy of not participating in the first place.

The movement of the squares overlapped with a very popular campaign against one of the most detested and iniquitous financial burdens placed upon ordinary Greeks arising from the neoliberal era of privatisation and of the austerity measures, which were an extension of it. *Non sipaga!*

My first experience of the 'can't pay, won't pay' movement was in the summer of 2010. Driving south with friends from Salonika (also referred to as Thessaloniki) to our holiday on the Pelion peninsula we came to a toll-booth. Eva promptly stopped the engine, got out of the car, walked up to the barrier, forced it up, got back in and off we drove – waving at the woman in the booth. She beamed a smile back. 'Err ... what just happened?' I asked. Eva replied, as the rest of the passengers laughed, 'Oh we don't pay. Not for the privatised tolls. The money goes straight to the oligarchs. It doesn't go to the public purse. That, of course, would be different.' Billions of euros went in to road construction in the boom years. Public money handed to private contractors to build and own the motorways – and to charge exorbitant tolls. As living standards collapsed, large numbers of hard-pressed people felt both a financial necessity and moral justification in refusing to pay the racketeers.

These two movements did much more than provide a field in which the often university-recruited activists of the radical left could engage with much wider forces than they were used to. Participation went beyond even the organised labour movement and included ruined small businessmen and the struggling self-employed – a large sector of the pre-crisis Greek workforce. The movements helped also to transform mass opinion over the decisive political question: what to do about the mountain of debt which was now, thanks to the bank bailouts, on the state's balance sheet?

At the end of 2010 there was broad consensus among the parliamentary parties that the debt had to be paid. Pasok and New Democracy would stick to the line that Greece would pay every single cent right up to the agreement they made in 2012 for a limited debt write-off in return for even harsher austerity. Syriza's initial position was to tax the rich to pay the national debt. Only a minority on the radical left – outside Syriza and some figures within, such as economist Costas Lapavitsas – argued that the debt was unpayable and that trying to pay it would lead to a 'debt trap', whereby sucking money out of the economy for debt repayments leads to recession. As the economy shrinks, the relative burden of the debt increases. That is exactly what happened over the next five years. Further, handing money to the European banking system was giving it back to the business class who were the ones who had been bailed out by the memorandum deal. And it was that which had left the public footing the bill in the first place.

The movements of 2011 shifted majority opinion, in society and the left, towards repudiating at least the 'odious debt', that is the portion run up profligately by corrupt previous governments. 'Can't pay, won't pay' provided a doable, individual instantiation of what collective refusal to pay the debts of the bankers and oligarchs might mean. The squares and associated popular assemblies provided both a credible portrait of the power such collective organisation could exercise and also an ongoing, organised debate in which refusing to pay the debt became majority sense. There were many hundreds of well-attended local meetings, right down to village level, at which left-wing speakers who were capable of explaining their ideas without a library of jargon found deep resonance for radical policies which pointed to a break with the whole economic logic of free market capitalism. We shall return to those arguments in more detail. The two most immediate consequences, however, were these. First, Syriza broke from the official consensus that the debt had to be paid one way or another. Its new policy sometimes oscillated between outright debt cancellation and some kind of inquiry to decide what was legitimate and what was odious. The speaker of the parliament, Zoe Konstan-topoulou, commissioned just such an inquiry upon taking office in 2015. Second, the shift over the debt issue brought to the foreground the question of the euro and membership of the EU.

The crisis in Greece and the strategic choice facing the Syriza government in 2015 have tended to be characterised as: in or out of Europe; euro or drachma (Greece's pre-euro currency)? The euro question did indeed figure centrally in how the pro-memorandum governments sought to make a coherent way forward for Greek capitalism and also to defuse popular resistance. They systematically deployed the threat of exiting the single currency as a weapon against the struggles of masses of people, who feared doing so even as they fought the consequences of what it means to remain inside. The euro was pivotal to the critical debates of early summer 2015, arising from the first few months of Syriza taking office and from the agreement it entered into for a third austerity memorandum, which are considered in this book's concluding chapter.

It would be a big mistake, however, to imagine that Europe and the euro were the starting point for those debates. There were some on the Greek left who had always – like a British Eurosceptic – maintained that EU membership and then the single currency were the source of all the country's woes. But they remained politically marginal even as the euro question moved centre-stage. And that happened as a result of the shift in mass sentiment over the more fundamental and pressing question of the debt. The way the major centres of the world economy dealt with the banking and private sector debt crisis following 2008 was to nationalise, to statify, the debt while leaving the means to make future profits in private hands. The state took on the banks' debts. The bankers kept their bonuses and control of the banks. When people in Greece repudiated the now state debt, in mass opinion and then at the polls by voting for Syriza, that brought them into a clash with the governments and elites of other states within the eurozone. The argument to break with the euro arose from the mass movements of people in 2011, which led them to reject the idea that they should pay the debts of the Greek business class and banks.

Pasok, New Democracy and the forces of the Greek business class well understood the logic and deployed it in reverse. If you are committed to a future in Europe, then you have to accept paying the debt and that means austerity. The polarised argument in Syriza and on the radical left did not come from the invoking of ideological shibboleths or dogmatic schemes by a part of the left with the intention of creating a row to justify their political choices. It is an unavoidable corollary to the courageous struggles of millions of Greek people to resist social ruination. And it is because those struggles were sustained that the dilemma of euro membership became more and more acute.

Moves to implement a second memorandum and round of austerity in October 2011 brought a further wave of mass strikes and militant street confrontation. They shattered the Papandreou government. On the national commemoration on 28 October – Oxi (No) Day – of Greece's rejection of Mussolini's ultimatum leading to the invasion of 1940, the Greek president and entourage were forced to abandon the parade in Salonika. Across the country protesters joined the parades and directed the 'national No' at their own government, not an external power. Papandreou had planned to hold a referendum in which the question would be posed in a way so as to use the majority opinion for staying in the euro as a lever to force through reluctant acceptance of the austerity, which was the hated price for doing so. European leaders blocked the plan. They told Papandreou, in effect and in the bluntest of language, to show the mettle of his father. Andreas had directly confronted his support among the Greek working class with a turn to austerity from 1985 onwards. Either that or little George was to make way for someone who would. Papandreou resigned and was replaced by a national unity government under a caretaker, unelected prime minister. In January 2012, some 43 Pasok and New Democracy MPs rebelled on the vote for the new memorandum which the new banker prime minister of Greece pushed through parliament.

Syriza headed towards new elections in May that year with Pasok in free fall and, as second placed party, running New Democracy very close. Its position of 'not one sacrifice for the euro' was susceptible to the argument that the euro demanded sacrifice. Pasok tried to run that line. But it had overseen two years of austerity and had little credibility left. A Pasok councillor in Patras, western Greece, and an old friend told me during the election campaign:

> I'm still just hanging on with the party. But my voters have gone. I've never seen anything like it. They smile at you, because they know you. But when you speak about voting for the old party they have supported for years it's like their ears are closed. They keep smiling at you, but it's like they have literally not heard a word you have said. I suppose it's only because I'm known as a party critic that I get even the smiles.

New Democracy majored on a much cruder and combative theme – civil war era anti-Communist witch-hunting and racism. The two elections of May and June 2012 confounded the nostrums of the 1990s – that you win an election by moderately appealing to the centre. For the captains of the old official parties, 'the centre' was invariably several degrees starboard of midships. Samaras narrowly won in both elections by galvanising the right. He lacked an overall majority. He formed a coalition government in June with Pasok and Dimar providing centrist ballast.

In June, New Democracy took 30 per cent, Syriza 27 per cent, Pasok 12 per cent and Dimar 6 per cent. Months of polling as second party had allowed Syriza credibly to fight the campaign with the message of 'for a government of the left'. The collapse of Pasok transformed what it meant to vote for Syriza. It was no longer an expression of solidarity with its ideas or of support for its untainted and likeable figures, such as Tsipras. If Syriza could outpoll New Democracy, then it was promising actually to govern with others on the left, opposed to austerity and for the first time bringing to office the historic left with traditions rooted in the radical history of twentieth-century Greece. It came agonisingly close. Despite coming first, New Democracy suffered a haemorrhaging of votes to its right. The Independent Greeks took 7.5 per cent, with 7 per cent for the fascist Golden Dawn. Both pitched themselves as national defenders of Greece against the 'foreign-imposed' austerity memorandums. The far right party LAOS, which had joined the earlier caretaker government, fell short of the 3 per cent threshold and was out of parliament. Indeed, every party which had implemented the memorandums lost support. The KKE had not. It was returned to parliament with 4.5 per cent but had been squeezed by a third of its voters switching to Syriza hoping to give it first place. Under the Greek electoral system at the time, coming first provided a bonus 50 seats out of 300 and the constitutional right to try to form a government after June.

The *ancien regime* had survived, but at great cost. In the salons of the complacent European elites and highly paid commentators, the insurgency was seen as having peaked. The government had a majority and would be strong. The historic animosities between its coalition components would be subordinated to pressing through the storm, then to disembark in calmer waters and restart the old political game. There was even a whiff of that among sections of the European left who bitterly pored over the entrails of the May and June elections, pointing the finger at one another for the narrow failure of the left to win outright. Without belittling the importance of those arguments, which at their more serious touched on the very question of how the left might actually hold power, too often they were conducted with the recrimination appropriate to the closing of an historical epoch with its opportunities missed. In fact, the actual success of the left pointed to an era of possibility and of widening horizons just opening up.

From 2012 to 2015

Samaras governed as he had campaigned: from the hard right and for the social layers that backed the old conservative right. Now in government, the old chauvinist charlatan had no wiggle room for opportunistic demurral from the euro-required and oligarch-desired austerity policies. He had to implement them. As the predicted results of those policies mounted, a smaller economy and therefore a higher debt burden, the permanent downward pressure on living standards fuelled a leftwards rejection of austerity policies in the minds of the mass of Greeks. Unable to base himself on a positive case for his economic policy, Samaras relied increasingly upon the authoritarian and racist rhetoric examined in chapter 4.

Syriza elaborated upon the logic of the slogan with which it had overtaken Pasok in the minds of working-class voters as the electoral alternative to New Democracy – 'for a government of the left'. Government meant wielding executive power. Especially in response to the kind of crisis Greece was in, that meant coherence, a degree of centralisation and decisiveness. At its conference in 2013 Syriza became a party. The component organisations of the previous coalition largely dissolved themselves into a more centralised structure.[11] The left of the new party became organised in what was called the Left Platform. It comprised the old left of Synaspismos, called the Left Current, and some of the 11 other, much smaller, organisations which had merged to form Syriza. The Left Platform won about a third of the congress delegates to its political positions and list of candidates for the party's executive, the 201-strong Central Committee. As it became clear to even the most recalcitrant of the corporate media 18 months later that Syriza was going to form the next government of a modern European country, there was much guffawing and bemusement that the new governing party had a *central committee*. That surely marked it out as a hangover of an antediluvian Communist past or a group of student revolutionists overreaching themselves. In fact, every party – including New Democracy – in Greece has a leading body called a central committee. Not only the Communist left, but the nationalist right had never abandoned the insight of the Russian revolutionary Lenin and his central committee that ideas without central organisation are politically impotent.

From 2013 to the January 2015 election, Syriza looked like a government in waiting. That brought additional pressures. The old bugbear of whether to adopt a junior partner status to Pasok had been slain thanks to the deserved collapse of that party, which did worse than prop up a government imposing austerity. That was to be expected. Until late 2013 Samaras's *chef de cabinet*, Takis Baltakos, was in secret negotiations with Golden Dawn leaders about some future compact. He and they hailed from the seedbed of the radical right in Greece, the conservative landowning class of the Mani peninsula on the Peloponnese. That the party of Andreas Papandreou was complicit, through its coalition with Samaras in parliament, was shocking even to the dwindling working-class base of Pasok, who had imagined their party to have long since drained the cup of treachery. But if not from Pasok, where else to seek political allies?

The answer from the most radical, anti-capitalist currents inside Syriza was to seek a government with the Communist Party, supported by the significant extra-parliamentary left. The KKE, which had easily defied silly predictions of its total collapse and was recovering from its squeezed vote of 2012, made clear that it would not be part of such a government. It justified that position to itself and its supporters with the kind of argument the left inside Synaspismos had put – with real justification – a few years earlier regarding Pasok: we want to replace you, why should we put ourselves in a subordinate relationship to you? In any case, the leading group around Tsipras, which comprised old figures from Synaspismos and some of Tsipras's generation, made a compelling alternative argument.

It tended to be advanced in the language of Marxist theory, which is more widely spoken in Syriza and on the left in Greece than anywhere else in Europe. Too often it was conducted in jargon. But when expressed popularly it amounted to this: with around 40 per cent (which was roughly the combined percentage achieved in 2015) the left cannot hope to govern successfully. It needs a majority in parliament and also in the country. We should seek to win that majority by dividing the right through tactical alliances with the more moderate elements, or with those who support our stance on the memorandum, against the more extreme opponents. The logic was similar to the strategy in 2010, which had lionised ex-Pasok figures. And it turned out to be just as impeccably mistaken.

In March 2013, Tsipras spoke at a meeting organised by the Karamanlis Institute, to mark the fifteenth anniversary of the death of the grand old man of the patrician Tory right. In his speech, Tsipras contrasted what in Britain might be called Karamanlis's 'one-nation Tory' vision with the hard right chauvinism pursued by Samaras. With these two heads of New Democracy stands a third – the Thatcherite, free market wing represented Dora Bakoyanni – together making up three-headed hell-hound Cerberus, which is the centre right. After the European elections in 2014, Tsipras decided that the left had a dog in the fight that erupted among Angela Merkel, David Cameron and the other austerity leaders in the EU. Citing convention and protocol, Tsipras backed Jean-Claude Juncker, the former right-wing prime minister of Luxembourg, to be president of the EC against German objections. There was no policy or principle at issue. Juncker was and has since proved to be wholly at odds with the anti-austerity position of Syriza and the radical left forces in Europe alongside whom it fought the European Parliament elections on a unified ticket. It was, rather, a signal to other European governments and to Juncker that a Syriza-led Greece would play by the rules. The hope, presumably, was that it would get credit for so doing. Juncker got the powerful position of president of the EC, one of the components of the Troika. He had already been given a bauble by the Greek state in recognition of his supposed phil-hellenism. Syriza got nothing, and Greek workers less than nothing when the EC continued to lock arms with the rest of the Troika and to squeeze Syriza once it was elected.

There were policy consequences to the strategy. By late 2014, the unstable holding position of 'not one sacrifice for the euro' had been abandoned – first in the speeches of leading figures, which defined actual policy to the media and public more than any conference resolution; then in a new form of words in party literature. Syriza was now committed to staying in the euro, but fighting to win within the European institutions a break from austerity. At the Ambrosetti beano by Lake Como, Italy, in late August 2014, Tsipras made that case to global chief executives and 'world leaders', couched in pro-business terms. A few days later at the annual protest by the Greek labour movement in Salonika, Syriza unveiled the programme it promised to implement in government to relieve the humanitarian crisis in Greece for the very poorest. It was a balancing act. Its fulcrum was, nevertheless, to the left of the European political class, who argued that there was no alternative to austerity and who were ideologically committed to 'reforming' further what was left of the social safety net, not patching it up. Syriza in government would face the excruciating contradiction between staying in the euro and resisting the austerity policies which are hardwired into it. A few months before, however, that paradox slapped Samaras in the face, setting in train the process which brought Syriza to office.

Samaras pleaded. He begged. The answer was no. All he was after was two months' grace and the release of a little of the funds yet to be disbursed under the second memorandum. He needed to get over the constitutional hurdle of getting through parliament with the support of 180 MPs his choice for the position of president of Greece.[12] The economy was finally turning, he said. While acknowledging his government had faltered in actually driving into the souls and guts of popular Greece measures it had passed on paper, he would do better. And he would do something about the scandalous level of tax evasion by the wealthy. He promised to. But the EU mandarins in Paris that October and November decided they would squeeze anyway. A confidant of Samaras's later told the paper *Kathimerini* 'when they finally said no, I knew the game was up'. The forensic detail of that moment is extraneous to this short account. But with the European crisis grinding on, punctuated by points of decision under extreme political pressure, this question is of more than academic or historical interest: how could the agents of the IMF and European capitalist elites misjudge so spectacularly? A part of the answer is surely the habitual thinking they have displayed throughout the deepest systemic crisis since the Second World War. Tomorrow will be an extension of yesterday through the whiling away of today. With this mentality they could reassure themselves that, although Syriza was ahead in the polls, the combined forces of New Democracy, Pasok and their satellites would surely win an election. Just like last time, the right's scare tactics would put it ahead, even if without an overall majority. In any case, there was still a pro-memorandum majority in parliament. It was heading into December and turkeys do not vote for Christmas: there were enough wavering forces for Samaras to scrape together the 180 MPs' votes he needed. A number of friends, from the opposite point of view, cited the decline in overt social struggle over the previous year as an unwelcome reason for the same assessment. But Samaras lost the vote between Christmas and New Year. He was forced to call the general election for 25 January.

Habit, too, informed his campaign: anti-Communist scaremonger-ing spiced with racism. In an admittedly crowded field, he plumbed the depths of official Europe's exploitation of the *Charlie Hebdo* atrocity, brazenly apportioning it to 'uncontrolled migration into Europe'. Having held a modest lead for months, but failing to elicit much enthusiasm with its moderating message, Syriza swung sharply left on day one of the campaign in response to Samaras. Extraor-dinarily, Tsipras launched his campaign saying that if elected his government would look to the support of the KKE and Antarsya. The KKE would definitely win seats. But Antarsya? What was the leader of a party leading the polls doing even mentioning a coalition of avowedly revolutionary groups which, though respected as activists, was very unlikely to poll over 3 per cent?

In making that statement – which he neither repeated nor disavowed during the rest of the campaign – the Syriza leader sent a message to a politically alert but wearied working-class electorate that a Syriza government was indeed going to be a break from the past. It would be of the left. In referencing the non-governmental parties of the left he echoed the contempt in which millions of people held the established time-servers. It worked. The reason: the underlying shift to the left in the expression of opinion in the Greek political system. That had been driven by enormous social struggles over five years and the way the radical left had participated in them, arguing for its ideas and for a new politics. One aspect of that was the rejection of a permanent capitulation to the right and abrogation of what you believe in through 'triangulation'. Under that voodoo politics, the left should seek a midpoint between itself and the right in order to win a middle ground. The result is to shift this fabled middle ever further to the right. As the British Labour Party demonstrated in May 2015, it is also to lose. Another aspect was to pose a very different relationship between the collective struggles of millions of people for control over their own lives and the new faces of the radical left to which they were prepared to transfer their old loyalties.

CHAPTER THREE

Their Austerity and Our Resistance

The IMF made a rare admission in 2013. It reported that its optimistic forecast for the results of Greece imposing the austerity policies it had insisted upon had proved wrong. Instead of a contraction of the economy of around 5.5 per cent, and then a recovery, Greece was heading for a 17 per cent fall in output. Wrong by a factor of three. Over the next two years further predictions of 'green shoots' of recovery were to prove just as inaccurate. The supposed recovery at the end of 2014 turned into contraction just three months later. Many economists have outlined in detail the scale of the economic collapse in Greece resulting from – or at least compounded by – the austerity memorandums, not least Syriza finance minister Euclid Tsakalotos, who took over from Yanis Varoufakis in July 2015.[13] In the face of those analyses, still more of the undisputable facts, the question is why government after government stuck to a policy which demonstrably failed. That, however, raises the issue of what it means to say that policy failed. Failed for whom? What was it intended to achieve?

Greece followed the global response to the onset of what was at first thought to be merely a crisis of the banks and financial system in 2008 and the state took on the private sector's debts. It was that which brought about the spiralling national debt, not some supposed overly generous welfare system or that Greeks had 'lived beyond their means'. The Greek welfare system was one of the most miserly in Europe. Greeks worked the longest hours in the EU. Wages were low. The only egregiously large state expenditure was on the military. By nationalising the private sector's debts, but leaving the profits in its hands, what was a crisis of free market capitalism took on the appearance of a crisis of the state budget and of a national emergency in which all would have to make sacrifices to pay down the astronomical debt. The right played on the imagery of national unity and 'honouring' the nation's debt obligations. One odd cultural resource was the ridiculous Hollywood film *300*, released in 2007 on the eve of the Great Recession. Ostensibly retelling the story of the heroic defence of the pass at Thermopylae by a small group of Spartan soldiers from the invading Persian army of King Xerxes, all it proved is that racist, misogynist drivel remains just that, no matter how much computer-generated imagery is applied. The defenders at Thermopylae in the fifth century BC were overcome thanks to the treachery of a local villager – a Greek by the name of Ephialtes. From his name comes the Greek word for nightmare. It was the Greek business class and its political allies who sold the contemporary pass and opened the way to the nightmare years of austerity. For the entire policy, far from being a foreign imposition from without, was for them a means to prosecute the kind of class war and shift in wealth from working people to the rich which they had tried but failed to accomplish in the period of neoliberal modernisation.

So the bailouts, the loans to the Greek state to ensure that it maintained debt repayments, meant that 90 per cent of the money went back into the Greek and European banking systems which had been the trigger for the crisis in the first place. The policies demanded in return by the Troika of lenders – slashing limited welfare and public spending, mass sackings, cutting wages by a third – were what Greek capitalism had been after ever since it was forced to head off the explosion of militancy following the fall of the Junta through a social compromise with the trade union leaderships, who in turn were to keep in check those left-wing forces fighting for much more. The national debt was a weapon for the Greek capitalist class to go much further than the modernising governments of the 1990s and early 2000s had been able to. It came as little surprise when the Greek equivalent of the *Times*, *Kathimerini*, ran a series of in-depth articles revealing that representatives of Greek big business had routinely sent secret requests to Troika negotiators to include in their demands of governments in Athens a string of measures such as abolishing the minimum wage, scrapping collective bargaining, making it easier to fire workers and so on. In a sense, the vindicated warnings of even mainstream economists that the austerity regime would tip the Greek economy over the cliff were beside the point. The purpose of the austerity measures was not economic well-being, it was to cement the position of European and Greek big business. The euro economic zone certainly favoured German big business. The currency was kept at a level benefiting German exports, even if it created recessionary pressures in the weaker economies of the south. But Greek business signed up to it, and remains wedded to it, because it was also a way to maintain permanent pressure on working people's living standards. For that was the main way big business sought to deal with declining profitability.

If we talk about the failure of austerity, the question is – failure for whom? Under the austerity regime, European big business has managed to inflict massive attacks on the continent's workforce, in most cases without facing the level of social unrest – up to mid 2015 at any rate – which they had feared. This is the fundamental reason why government after government in Greece stuck to the policy, even as they tried to negotiate with the Troika around the edges. It is also why Greek business, despite the economic collapse, demanded more of the same. For all the talk of national emergency, the Hellenic Business Federation in spring 2015 publicly undermined the efforts of the Syriza-led government to reach any deal with the Troika which night mitigate further attacks on pensions and workplace rights.

The establishment's consensus around the class war policy of austerity was the reason why a gulf opened up between it and the mass of Greek people, resulting in wave after wave of social resistance examined below. But it also meant a social disaster. The impact of the crisis years on Greek society is now widely known. Here I want to focus on what it meant for young people in particular. In part, because it is among the young that the left's growth was most pronounced and also where the creative possibilities of a radically new politics are most developed.

To be young in a time of crisis

To atone for his crime, Aegeus, the ruler of Athens, was compelled every seven or nine years to offer up from the city's youth a sacrifice to King Minos of Knossos on Crete. They were to be devoured by his monstrous half-man, half-bull secured inside the labyrinth below the Cretan royal palace. The story seems today a premonition in ancient myth of the modern boom–slump business cycle. History recalled truly as James Joyce's nightmare from which we are trying to awake. The Great Recession hit all strata of Greek society outside of the oligarchic 1 per cent. None suffered more than the young.

Electoral support for Syriza and for the left as a whole soared among younger voters as the economic crisis ripped through Greek society. The correlation of voting pattern to age in 2015 was stronger even than to social class. New Democracy enjoyed most of the support among those aged over 55. In all the younger age-groups, the left polled over-whelmingly. One of the many violations of democracy committed by the Samaras government was as a final act to disenfranchise tens of thousands of first-time voters. This conscious culling of the youth vote compounded the blind processes of the slump itself in striking from the voter lists supporters of the left. From 2008 to Syriza's election victory some 200,000 young people left Greece in search of work abroad. Talk of a 'lost decade' for them is not some macro-economic statistic of flat-lining national economic output. Even for economics students in Greece it is more than a salutary warning from 1990s Japan of the damage done by deflating an economy through balancing budgets and imposing austerity when the opposite policy is called for, of the kind Keynes had urged 1930s policy makers to adopt. For those in their twenties, a lost decade is all of their adult life. The social impact of that is enormous – and cumulative. A decade or more of lost life chances is not recovered. It is consolidated into every succeeding year. It is impossible to grasp the contours and trajectory of radical politics in Greece without understanding that social impact and its reflexes in political ideas, parties and attachments.

The usual international measures of youth unemployment are for the 16–24-year-old age range. Unemployment rates in this group remained over 50 per cent in 2015. In the 15–19-year-old age range they stood at 56 per cent for males and 79 per cent for females in 2012 and barely declined with what were hailed as the first shoots of recovery three years later.

A study by David Bell and David Blanchflower published in January 2015[14] made a convincing case for broadening the impact of youth unemployment to include the 25–29-year-old cohort. Many of them left school or university in the crisis years. Their rates of unemployment are lower than those of teenagers, but the study found that:

> Despite the fact that the unemployment rate for 25 to 29 year olds was only 57 per cent of that for 15 to 19 year olds, there were 7.7 unemployed persons aged 25–29 for each unemployed person aged 15–19 in 2012. And the absolute numbers unemployed in the 25–29 age group (222,000) exceeded the number unemployed in the entire 16–24 age group (173,000) by 28 per cent.

The lower unemployment rates of those in their late twenties can almost wholly be explained by net emigration of this age group from Greece. The more mobile among that age group tend to be the better educated. Those left behind are disproportionately from the poorer layers of Greek society. The other great skew in the youth unemployment figures on the wider age range is by gender. The popular image of 'disaffected youth' in Greece is of black-clad, nihilistic young men in hoodies fighting with the police and smashing up banks. In reality, it is young women who have suffered higher rates of soul-destroying unemployment. The left's share of the vote is also significantly higher among them than among young men. The movement which erupted in the summer of 2015 against a third austerity memorandum was disproportionately working-class, young and female.

One pervasive feature of life for the young which has defrayed some of the economic hardship of unemployment is the extraordinarily high rate of staying on in the parental home, often into their thirties. It cannot be explained by some presumed traditionalism of family ties with a consequent delayed sense of adulthood. Greece has compulsory one-year male national service. That clearly obliges temporary departure from the family home to the barracks, but then most young men return. Early into the crisis there was much anecdotal evidence of couples in their thirties with young children moving back into one or other parental home. According to one study:

> only one out of three 25 to 29 year olds in Greece live away from home, whereas in the UK, four out of five have left home. In part, this is likely to reflect lack of jobs but also in part the inflexibility of the housing market … [T]he highest home ownership rates in the OECD are in Spain and Greece; unemployment appears to be positively correlated with home ownership rates.[15]

It goes on to suggest that the expansive home ownership market, which was so championed by neoliberal policy makers in Greece and was a staple of modernising aspirations from the 1960s onwards, has led to 'a lack of a private rental sector that allows young people to move to where the jobs are'.

That presupposes that there are such jobs, at the so-called entry level of lower pay, greater insecurity and zero-hours contracts. In fact, though young women are more likely to live away from home than young men, female unemployment rates are significantly higher than male ones. That does not suggest a generation of young people fed on state-welfarism and unprepared to leave the nest, get on their bikes and find a job.

'Get on yer bike' was the infamous response of Thatcherite hard man Norman Tebbit to the epidemic of youth unemployment in Britain brought by the crisis of the early 1980s and the British government's deliberate policy of driving up the jobless rate to provide advantageous ground for the neoliberal offensive. Tebbit's provocation vividly popularised for the neoliberal right the more prosaic free market economists' doctrine of the 'supply side revolution'. The problem was not a lack of jobs, which may be solved by increasing aggregate demand and creating them. It was some propensity of the jobless to be unemployed. That was to be solved by 'removing labour market rigidities' – cutting wages, savaging shopfloor union organisation, slashing legal employment protection and anything else which led to young people 'pricing themselves out of a job'.

Two decades on, crisis-wracked Greece provided a laboratory for such measures – with the younger generations serving as lab rats. The neoliberal dogma was tested to *their* destruction. Youth unemployment on all measures remained impervious to every 'liberalisation' of the labour market. Successive governments scrapped the minimum wage, made it easier for employers to sack workers *en masse*, squeezed an already emaciated welfare benefits system and heaped every imaginable social and psychological pressure on young people to 'get on their bikes'. Those who could not get on a budget flight to find work in another country continued to find themselves without even the prospect of a job.

There is little evidence from the literature that [these policies] work, especially in a recession where over a quarter of the labour force and over a half of the youth labour force are unemployed. This is unprecedented territory when overall unemployment is so high and an immediate expansion in aggregate demand is precluded.[16]

⌈This generation has inherited a double, bitter legacy. Not only are young people the victims of the failed economic policies. The young also see slipping from them the greater autonomy and social freedoms which the champions of neoliberal modernisation at the turn of the millennium claimed were more than compensation for a necessary precarity in modern employment. To borrow the terminology of left-wing French sociologist Pierre Bourdieu, who was an early and elegant critic of the great claims of capitalist globalisation and a major influence on the *altermondialiste* or anti-capitalist movement in the early 2000s: it is not just that the 'left hand of the state' (post-war welfarism) has retreated from serving the social good; it is also that the 'right hand', its repressive and coercive apparatuses, has reached deeper into society, gasping the throat of, above all, the young.⌋

The rebalancing of the state to promote the economically neoliberal and the socially illiberal in the crisis years in Greece brought not only the kinds of petty diktat, authoritarian rhetoric, and imposition of traditional social mores against which generations of students and young people had bridled ever since the fall of the Junta in 1974. It also closed in on their lives, foreshortening their future. Literally.

Alexis Grigoropoulos would have been 21 years old in January 2015 and of the generation which, when not voting Syriza was quite likely to cast a vote for the KKE or for the anti-capitalist Antarsya coalition. But he was killed on 6 December 2008 – shot dead at the age of 15 by two policemen. The youth uprisings across Greece which followed were larger than anything seen for four decades. That rebellion is the first of the sites of social resistance we examine.

The 2008 uprising

The intensity of the street fighting, its duration and geographical spread rivalled the 2005 riots in France, triggered when two teenagers in Clichy-sous-Bois, Bouna Traoré and Zyed Benna, were electrocuted after running from the police and taking refuge in an electricity substation. Unlike the French events, or the black-led inner city riots in Britain in 1981, the 2008 youth rising was not focused in ethnic minority areas. It reached into even small towns of a couple of thousand inhabitants in rural Greece. There was one 'immigrant' dimension, however. For the first time the children of Albanian, South Asian and African immigrants did the Greek militant thing of hurling stones at police stations, torching expensive cars and setting up ramshackle barricades. I spoke with some in Nikea, a poor area of western Athens, mid riot that Christmas holiday. Marenglen, aged 17, whose parents moved to Greece from Albania in 1996, said:

> There is nothing for us. Nothing. My brother is in prison. We are harassed all the time by the police. And now they have killed this lad in Exarcheia. Do not think it is just the politicos who are rising up. The ones in black with their anarchy symbols. Look at us. We are just kids. But our lives count. We will make them hear us …

With that, he headed off with a group of friends all his age, Greek and Albanian, armed with some rather expertly made Molotov cocktails.

Like France's Jacques Chirac in 2005 and Britain's Margaret Thatcher in 1981 before him, New Democracy Prime Minister Costas Karamanlis tried to summon a 'silent majority' backlash. I remember the oligarch-owned television channels endlessly looping the pitiful image of the national Christmas tree. It had been erected proudly outside the parliament on Syntagma Square. Almost immediately it was torched and burnt to cinder. But already in *laiki*, popular Greece, the chill winds from the financial crash that year were beginning to cut into the budgets of households which had, in the previous decade, made up for soaring food prices (due both to an overnight inflation hike which came with the introduction of the euro and to the worldwide rise in the costs of agricultural production), rising housing costs and stagnant wages by resort to unsecured credit. Just as in Britain, Ireland and in the Spanish state. A surprising number of people were in no mood to relish a round of youth sacrifice on the altar of law and order. The burnt-out Christmas tree already stood as a portent of economic hard times for many more than those who saw it as a symbol of national embarrassment.

A further factor undermined attempts to blame the rioting on feral youth, led astray by sinister anarchists. The successful university and high school occupations of 2006–7 had led large numbers of young people towards the activist left. It also had a social impact as many parents viewed the struggle sympathetically.

The Communist Party's youth organisation, KNE, had refreshed its base in the student movement. It was very strong among under-graduates. So was the Antarsya coalition, as well as large anarchist and autonomist tendencies. Syriza's strength was more among older postgraduates, PhD students in particular. The response of KKE general secretary Aleka Papariga to the uprising, however, revealed the conservatism at the heart of the party's leadership, despite its ultra-radical rhetoric. She denounced the rioters and hinted at the work of unnamed provocateurs. With words which would later be thrown back at young Communist loyalists she contrasted the 'anarchist chaos' to what a properly proletarian revolution would look like. 'In our revolution,' she said, 'not a single pane of glass will be broken.' Not for the first time the youth of a party which prided itself on its leadership of the heroic (and more than glass-shattering) war of national liberation against the Nazis were left in confused paralysis.

The forces of the revolutionary and anti-capitalist left, by and large, had no difficulty showing solidarity with the revolt – though a few who hailed from the orthodox Communist tradition felt the lure of old instincts, contrasting properly organised struggles to 'anarchist adventures'. That meant that there was a pole of the political, Marxist left on the streets vying with the anti-authoritarian anarchist or autonomist strands whose jib seemed to catch more easily the wind of street confrontation. What was the position of Syriza?

Its recently elected young leader Alexis Tsipras defied those within the coalition and its main component Synaspismos whose instinct was, while naturally voicing some concern at the conditions of life for young people, firmly to distance the party from disorder. Tsipras and the group around him expressed clear sympathy for the youth in revolt. There was an enormous outcry in the media. It was not that Syriza was advocating street confrontation or armed overthrow of the state. It was not and never has. What it had done was to break the official, parliamentary consensus which was, ranging from the KKE to New Democracy, unequivocal in denouncing the riots and supporting the police. Many older and more conservative heads in the party urged a U-turn. Some did so publicly. Tsipras, however, and the leader of the parliamentary group, Alavanos, continued to hold a line which set the party at odds with the big battalions of the left and centre left. At the time Syriza had 14 MPs; the KKE, 22; and Pasok, 102.

The riots, as is their nature, subsided. The economic crisis hit and at the October 2009 election there seemed nothing to show for Tsipras's stand over the December uprising, except, perhaps, a vindication of the right within Synaspismos, who claimed that it was responsible for a slight drop in Syriza's vote. What it had done, however, was to create a relationship between Syriza – on one level, a party which did the conventional thing of standing in elections – and large numbers of young people, many of whom did the anti-conventional thing of participating in the violent youth revolt. That meant that the radical left became a reference point for those layers even if they did not immediately join it or vote for it. Strategically, it provided a bridge between two currents, both hit hard by the crisis but often divergent: the more traditional organised labour movement and left on the one hand, and radicalised young people often with a common sense of anti-political-party, vaguely anarchist ideas on the other. In so doing, it strengthened those inside Syriza and the rest of the radical left who saw fighting elections as a part of wider strategy for change, one which had at its centre the kind of social resistance and revolt of which the youth uprising proved to be an inchoate anticipation.

The workers' movement

The first big general strike against austerity and the Troika took place on 5 May 2010. It was massive. The General Confederation of Greek Workers (GSEE) is like the British Trade Union Congress, but for unions in the private sector. The equivalent in the public sector is called ADEDY. The GSEE-called strike surprised most people. For many years the federation had been under the control of Pasok. The strike was against a Pasok government signing up to the first austerity memorandum. The union leaders saw no alternative to a Pasok government, but felt the pressure from their own members to call the strike. It was the first of over 30 such general stoppages – in the private and public sectors – over the next five years. It might have been, if not the last, then one of far fewer.

On the Athens demonstration on the strike day, ritualistic anarchist fire-starting led to tragedy. A branch of the Marfin bank was set alight. Despite appearances, it was not empty. The management had locked in the workforce for the day. Three bank workers were killed in the fire. The right wing, its press and the government feasted on the deaths in an effort to derail movement. I was in Athens in the immediate aftermath as the establishment sought to whip up a lynch mob atmosphere. Those anarchist elements who pride themselves on confrontation with the police and authority ran for cover. Predictably. The official leaders of the movement spent more time denouncing the anarchists than taking about why half a million people had taken to the streets of Athens against the government. While not for a moment defending the fire-starting, friends on the radical left took to the streets, union meetings and airwaves defending the movement and pointing out that the bank had locked workers in, that the austerity policies were themselves murderous, that the government was trying to use the death of working people for political ends. It was a minority position at first. A friend of mine, Petros Constantinou, a radical member of the Athens city council and a leading figure in the anti-fascist movement, remains a bogeyman on the extreme right for his political defence of the movement. On the right of the spectrum the lie stuck that it was he who had started the fire. But Petros and that militant minority persisted and convinced more and more people. That, combined with the unrelenting attacks which the memorandum brought, meant that the movement was not thrown back. It continued, but with a larger core of people who themselves became more confident to articulate a response at future crisis points to those who sought to divide and confuse the movement.

That was a vital gain. For although the union federations could be pressured to call one-day general strikes (on occasion two days) they saw these as demonstrative. They were protests against what the government was doing. They were not accompanied by any plan to pose an alternative to the government or to extend the industrial action to the point where the country became ungovernable. The rise of Syriza to become a potential government in 2012 and then the actual government in 2015 did offer an alternative – replacing the old parties of government with the new. The wave upon wave of strikes – there were one-day general strikes every month and a half throughout 2011 – also developed another alternative. It was apparent not so much in the set-piece, one-day strikes, but in the plethora of indefinite strikes and in some cases workplace occupations, including at one point of government ministries. In those prolonged struggles there appeared notions of popular, worker control and decision-making as an alternative to being governed in the old way. Those ideas also flickered through hundreds of local community struggles and the movement of the squares in 2011.

The occupation of the squares

There is an historical irony in the internationalist imitation in Greece of the tactic of occupying public squares and spaces which spread from Egypt's Tahrir Square to the Spanish state and on to London,

New York and other cities. The Spanish movement in May 2011 was most extensive. Out of it came the anti-establishment party Podemos. By 2015 it was challenging the twin pillars of the Spanish party political system in the run-up to the general election at the end of the year. The Spanish squares movement adopted the name '_los indignados_' – the indignant or outraged: citizens who had had enough of the outrageous, self-serving behaviour of the political and business elites. The Greek movement translated the name – _aganaktismenoi_ means the indignant ones in Greek. That had also been the term, however, for the shadowy forces of the violent nationalist right over the decades. It had sought to cover its carefully planned assaults on the left, including murder, as merely the work of citizens outraged, indignant at the Communist traitors to the nation. The connotations of the term in Greece certainly provided an excuse for a section of the left not to participate in a movement which was both beyond their control and unfamiliar in its form and tactics.

The squares movement was not a right-wing rabble, as the Communist Party and some others saw it. Neither was it, however, a movement spontaneously embracing the organised left. It began at the end of May 2011 with a common sense that was hostile to the participation of all political parties – including of the left. Given that it was the left which participated in 'street politics' that tended to mean especially the left. There was also hostility to the trade unions, held to be defenders of a sectional interest and tied to Pasok and the old political machines. The movement grew enormously in the first two weeks of June. It comprised large numbers of unemployed, self-employed, some small businessmen and others – some constituencies way beyond those the radical left had been used to addressing. The initial hostility to the left provided considerable space for right-wing ideas and even for activists from the far right posing as ordinary citizens. Nevertheless, the radical left participated and contested the ground.

The movement was opposed to the further austerity measures the Pasok government was about to pass. It also exposed the huge democratic deficit which allowed a government, acting in the name of the nation, to pass policies which the majority of the nation were demonstrably opposed to. The squares occupations were continuous, in Athens and in many other cities and towns. The permanent assembly of people went beyond a protest, a demonstration of opposition to an unpopular policy. It gave physical expression to the idea that popular assemblies, much more responsive to the views of the mass of people, were perhaps a more democratic way of doing things than through parliamentary elections for 300 MPs. That vague sentiment was compatible with all sorts of ideas about what 'the people' meant. Right-wing, xenophobic forces sought to project the idea that it meant the 'ethnically' Greek people, irrespective of class, against foreign enemies and excluding immigrant communities. The participation and arguments of left-wing activists were crucial. Without them taking up arguments against xenophobia and racism, constantly pointing to the fact that there were two 'nations' in Greece – the still rich oligarchy and the working masses – then there was indeed a danger, under a Pasok government, that right-wing populist forces or worse could have come to lead the movement. The decisive turning point came in the middle of June when the squares movement united with trade union demonstrations called to mark a one-day general strike. The combined impact of that and protests over the following days was to hamstring the Papandreou government. It limped on until November. The movement eventually subsided. But it had involved millions at its peaks and had had a powerful impact on mass thinking. It had challenged the idea, even if momentarily, that there was no other way of doing things than to have a parliament and government removed from the mass of people. There was a glimpse in the squares of an alternative, participatory democracy. It had been ruthlessly attacked at various points by the police. Bankrupt small businessmen, who had probably thought the police were doing a good job when they attacked left-wing protesters, now found themselves on the receiving end of tear gas and baton rounds. Some of the barriers between the radical left and people who tended to regard themselves as non-political were broken down, even though we were all separated in that square by the police lines and barriers from the parliament on its eastern side.

At the same time, the squares had shown how right-wing populist, even far right racist ideas could gain a hearing, especially as the dominant image on much of the left as well as the right was of Greece fighting for national survival. That could quickly turn to scapegoating and racism. The most significant counter to that was the united action with the trade unions in June, which provided a different sense of what 'the nation' represented – a working-class Greece in opposition to the Greece of the oligarchic business class. Immigrant organisations were on those protests. The experience of direct action and of participatory democracy of the squares also informed many militant local struggles.

Keratea and Skouries

Two of the most militant local struggles of the period arose from popular opposition to environmental destruction. For nearly 20 weeks spanning 2010 into 2011 the small town of Keratea near Athens became the site of militant civil disobedience by the inhabitants and against the authorities. The issue was a decision to extend the landfill site in the area, which served the huge greater Athens metropolis, even though the existing one had already disfigured people's lives. Keratea erupted in a truly popular protest. The municipal council, young people, their teachers, the entire community including priests joined daily battles with the police and the construction company hired to dig the site.

The media could not occlude the breadth of active support in the town for the protests. There were even pictures broadcast of priests blessing Molotov cocktails as young people hurled them niftily towards the construction machinery. The struggle was something other local communities could relate to. Coverage of the confrontation between residents of a small town on the one hand, and on the other corporate vandals and the remote city authority administration for Athens, framed the widespread feeling across the country that this was a battle of the little person against the big machine. It struck at the corrupt alliance between private contractors and municipal barons. The struggle succeeded in mitigating the damage to the local environment, though not in imposing a green, non-corporate solution. Importantly, it inspired many other areas to turn to collective action and to reproduce locally the militancy displayed in the national battles against austerity. Skouries is one such area. On the Halkidiki peninsula in northern Greece it became the battleground between local people and a Canadian mining conglomerate, Eldorado. (And they say North Americans don't get irony.) It also showed sharply how even the most local of struggles, in the general context of austerity, would raise more general questions which the movement would have to answer or find being used against it. If the Canadian mining firm's environmentally devastating expansion in Skouries was to be halted, what about the miners who faced losing their jobs if the company followed through on its threat to pull out of its existing operation?

Answering that meant creating an alternative, sustainable economic plan for the area. It also meant trying to break the company's hold on the workforce, which was so great it could use them to attack local protests. The local protests were not some alternative path to the national or to confronting the big political questions. On the contrary, countless community struggles pushed those big questions down to local level and into areas which people had thought separate from the politics of resistance to austerity. Above all, they brought additional layers of people into a process of collective struggle and of different ways of imagining how everything, from refuse disposal to the national economy, might be organised and run.

The ERT occupation and workers' control

By 2013 the Samaras government believed it had weathered the worst of the storm. Pro-government commentators consoled themselves that the peak of the social revolt appeared to be behind them. The governing coalition – New Democracy, Pasok and Dimar (the pro-market split from Synaspismos/Syriza) – appeared to give the administration a solid parliamentary majority and some breadth of support in society. Then, in June, the government moved to implement a further round of cuts. They included moving towards mass sackings of those with permanent contracts in local government and the wholesale closure of the national television and radio broadcaster, ERT – equivalent of the BBC in Britain. The reaction by the 2,500 ERT employees shook the government and ended its complacency. They occupied the central building in Athens and regional offices and broadcasting studios across the country. And they kept broadcasting, now with different news values.

The popular reaction was instantaneous. The government's treatment of the workforce had been brutal. It avoided the process of making people redundant by simply declaring the enterprise closed. In its place was a new, much smaller operation to be called NERIT. Workers would have to apply for new jobs there. The Samaras government was giving a lead to private sector employers as to how it should be done. It was also giving a present to the private media barons by, in effect, removing the national broadcaster from being any kind of competition. Within 24 hours thousands of people had begun rallying outside the offices in solidarity with the work-in. The pressure for a common front against the government brought a united effort by the parties of the left. At the first rally, the first speaker was from Syriza, followed by the Communist Party and then Antarsya. The forces of the left played a significant role over the next two years of the ERT struggle. But the initiative had come from the workforce itself. Days before the closure announcement a union meeting of the media workers' Prospert union, traditionally strongly under Pasok control, discussed what to do about the impending attack. A workplace rep who was also a member of Antarsya suggested that they occupy. He received one vote for the proposal. His own. Days later the workers did occupy. It was an answer to those who had claimed that the reserves of working people to resist had been drained.

For a few weeks over that summer there was a visible illustration of how people could not only resist, but also had the potential power to take control of the running of vital areas of the social services network, administration and economy. Already, across Greece there had been many social solidarity initiatives in which, for example, health workers – often unemployed due to cutbacks – would volunteer their time in improvised clinics to ensure that people got primary care. Now, by occupying the offices and studios they had been sacked from, rather than by setting up a pirate station from elsewhere, and then broadcasting under their own control, the ERT workers were taking that experiment a stage further. Soon delegations of other workers turned up – workers from a cement works, a bread factory, municipalities, where they were also on either extended strike or had occupied. They were interviewed by the occupying staff. Strikers, anti-racist campaigners, activists from the left were afforded the usual courtesies and time on air, which are normally reserved for establishment politicians. As a friend who works as a cook in a hospital told me:

We've seen 40 per cent of staff sacked at my hospital. Elsewhere hospitals have been closed completely. I know people who've been sacked who now volunteer in the social solidarity movement to provide rudimentary healthcare for those who can't access it. Of course, I applaud that. People outside of Greece should support it. But ERT is showing us something else. Something more important. Working people should not have to rely on a volunteer health service. It should be a national service, free and with all the medicines, instruments and staff required. You don't get that on a volunteer basis from sacked doctors and nurses. You get it by taking over the hospitals.

The government naturally moved very quickly to break the example set at ERT. It used brute force to evict the occupiers from the headquarters in Athens. But it was unable to do so across the whole of the country. And Samaras's administration was directly wounded too. Under huge pressure and now fighting for its life in anticipation of the next general election, Dimar left the coalition. It did not mean much in terms of votes in parliament – though thanks to defections the government majority was becoming perilously small. But it did further isolate the government in society. It was now just the two-faced beast of the established government parties, New Democracy and Pasok. The ERT struggle brought down one coalition and set the clock ticking on what remained. Then the eruption of the anti-fascist movement in September in response to the murder of Pavlos Fyssas forced the government further onto the back foot.

The occupations and exercise by workers of control over production and administration were a minority experience of the movement. The ERT struggle, however, did not peter out. Remarkably, the workforce – or the bulk of it which had not gone over to the NERIT replacement – continued to occupy and broadcast via internet. There were several consequences. The 'free ERT' broadcasting operation was a great asset for the movement. There was professional and in-depth coverage of the anti-fascist movement and other struggles. The core group of workers, who had shocked the government by occupying, stayed together through the work-in. That meant the lessons and experiences were not dissipated. Instead, these workers went on to develop innovative ways of organising the production of shows, challenging previous distinctions between technical and creative roles. It was hard. They were not being paid. So it was not a model for withdrawing from the society. Rather, it was a lived experiment of how democratic participation and control might be extended deeper into the society

– if the central structures of economic and state power were brought under control. The ERT workers maintained their work-in while also, like most other working people, looking to the election of a Syriza government to break the logjam. Syriza promised reinstatement. Three of the Syriza MPs elected in 2015 were ERT employees. By continuing their struggle, the ERT workers ensured that they had some leverage over what that reinstatement would look like. In May 2015 Syriza did re-open ERT. The workforce went in all together on day one, rather than the staggered return which the government had planned. While naturally welcoming reinstatement, they were in no mood to accept just anything on offer. There were unresolved issues over what to do about those who had scabbed on the struggle and gone over to the NERIT broadcaster. A major issue was the government's decision to re-employ as managing director the hated boss who had handed out the sacking notices and was known to be in favour of the memorandum-era style of management. A bitter cartoon criticising that decision appeared in the pages of *Avgi*, Syriza's daily paper. Workers said they would not accept his appointment. They also insisted on maintaining the collaborative ways of working they had developed over 18 months of struggle.

What was achieved?

Because it was so high-profile and was maintained over a long period, the ERT struggle was more than just one strike among many. It carried over into the new era of the Syriza government a minority experience in the struggle against its predecessors. Many people wondered – looking back on the dozens of general strikes, the occupations of the squares, the anti-racist movement and other struggles – what had been achieved. The traditional Pasok-style answer was that those kinds of struggles really showed why you needed to have a new government – us. Pasok was long past the point where it could play that game.

The struggles certainly ran up against definite limits. The general strikes raised the issue of going further with longer strikes. But that presupposed having a plan to keep vital services, such as hospitals and transport, going. Even the more local struggles, such as in Skouries, raised political questions, such as the organising of an alternative, sustainable economy for the area. One answer to those questions was to look to the election of Syriza – to give the left a chance for the first time ever. A second, minority, answer was provided fleetingly at the highpoints of the struggles themselves – developing new forms of democracy, challenging the old power centres for control, from the local environment to the national broadcaster.

For most people the two answers were not in opposition. And the fact that they coexisted in people's experience meant that the relationship between Syriza and its voters was not the same as it was for the old parties as the 2015 election approached. Hundreds of thousands of voters had switched allegiance from Pasok to Syriza. But they had not done so from the isolation of their living rooms, watching the performance of leading figures from both parties and judging accordingly. They had done so through the course of five years of struggles. In the course of participating in those struggles, they had come across the activists of the radical left, often for the first time. They had heard arguments which made sense – that the debt should be repudiated, that the immigrants were not to blame, that it was possible to bring down the government through collective struggle and so on. It remained an open question, after polling day, to what extent people had drawn the more radical conclusions of the previous years. But it was certainly the case that a lot more had taken place in Greek society than the old way of doing politics, with a fresh and much more honest choice of party on offer.

To some extent that was evident in the course of the election campaign itself. The fraught atmosphere on the left of 2012 had lifted. Syriza was ahead in the polls throughout the campaign. Under the Greek electoral system that meant that voting for any party of the left would not cost the left as a whole the chance of forming a government. So a space opened up on the left for serious discussion at grassroots level among the different forces contesting the election. That was especially so in the larger workplaces. If the national share of the vote for the left was around 42 per cent, in workplaces it was well over 60 per cent. Many of those voting for Syriza expressed sympathy for the arguments of the anti-capitalist left not in the party, which were in effect to generalise the experience of the high points of the struggle, such as at ERT, as well as, of course, voting left to get the Samaras government out. The years of struggle had done more than create a mass vote for a party of the left. At the base of those struggles, and among the activists of the left, new conversations about what was possible and new experiences of common action had been created, irrespective of which party people were in. Irrespective, also, of their national or ethnic backgrounds, despite Herculean efforts to convince them otherwise.

CHAPTER FOUR

The Monstrous Legacy of Racism

As the impact of the Great Recession ripped into the legitimacy of one government after another, leading figures in the political class turned to racist scapegoating. It provided a mechanism to win support and provide a false narrative which might appeal to those for whom the supposed virtues of austerity were non-existent.

The rise of xenophobia and racism was not restricted to Greece in the years following the collapse of Lehman Brothers. It was a Europe-wide phenomenon. That led to a rather one-sided and truncated observation, which had traditionally come from the left, becoming something of a journalistic commonplace. Hard economic times produce extremist racist movements of the right. So went the description masquerading as explanation. The sweeping generalisation had two weaknesses. First, it tended to naturalise what were in fact social and political developments, giving them the supposed force of a law of natural science. Just as a meteorological depression brings bad weather, so its economic equivalent brings a reactionary political climate. As well as an unjustified fatalism – why should a crisis of free market capitalism not give rise to a resurgence of left, collectivist alternatives? – it served secondly to exculpate those responsible for promoting racist ideologies, policies, interventions and movements. Racism is about more than individuals with racist ideas. It is structured into society and permeates the functioning of institutions. But racism and social structures are not borne aloft of their own accord or by other structures. They are embodied and transmitted by people.

The most visible and direct proponents of racialised politics in Greece are, of course, the neo-Nazis of Golden Dawn. In the two elections of 2012 they were catapulted into the Greek parliament. They emerged from the June election with just shy of 7 per cent, 426,025 votes and 18 MPs. In 2009 the list headed by veteran fascist and Golden Dawn leader Nikolaos Michaloliakos had barely registered with 19,636 votes and 0.29 per cent. The breakthrough over the next three years cannot be accounted for by some extraordinary genius on the part of the fascists or by some supposed, but unexplained, sudden propensity of the Greek population to hold hardened racist and chauvinist ideas. We shall return to how the fascists were able to exploit and grow from the consuming political crisis which attended the imposition of the austerity memorandums. But the racialisation of politics, the turning to explicitly xenophobic and ethnicised explanations of the social catastrophe engulfing working people in Greece, did not begin with Golden Dawn's breakthrough. Extremist racism was generated in the first instance not from the extreme right, but from a centre – from politicians and parties of government – which became more extreme the more the policy of savage austerity undermined its legitimacy. Indeed, the first indications of a growing salience of anti-immigrant and anti-Muslim racism within the mainstream came some years before the economic crisis ripped into an already creaking political order

Pakistani Greeks

In the late summer of 2005 a scandal erupted in Greece, which was to end up dogging not only the government of Costas Karamanlis, but also of the recently re-elected Tony Blair in Britain. It emerged that, in the days following the 7 July terrorist bombings of the London transport system, the Greek police and secret services had abducted 28 Pakistani immigrants in Athens and the north-western city of Ioannina. They had illegally detained and tortured them, allegedly in the presence of a British MI6 officer and at the behest of the British authorities. I spoke that autumn in Athens at a press conference hosted by the Greek anti-war movement and addressed by, among others, Javed Aslam, the leader of the Pakistani community organisation in Athens then representing 30,000 people.

The British, Greek and Pakistani governments all steadfastly rejected the claims as fanciful. By the middle of 2006 they had been forced to accept that, at the very least, the thrust of the story was indeed true.[17]

The Greek state prosecutor in May 2006 recommended that charges be brought against two Greek intelligence officers. The MI6 head of station in Athens had already been named in December of 2005 by the muckraking paper *Proto Thema* and had been spirited back to London where the Labour government issued a gagging order to prevent the media revealing his identity – a futile gesture in the age of the internet. Throughout 2006, and working in the parliamentary office of George Galloway , who was MP for the area in east London where one of the 7/7 bombers had struck, we fired a barrage of questions at Foreign Secretary Jack Straw about the case. What emerged in London and in Athens was not only the kind of state conspiracy which, in Greece as in the Middle East, the public imagination thrives upon thanks to a history of anti-democratic and extra-legal intrigues by the security state apparatus and the political right. Also apparent was the process, which had already been unleashed following the 9/11 attacks in the US, of a state-led and concerted ramping up of Islamophobic rhetoric to justify what would become wholesale abrogation of the rule of law and sanctity of individual liberty.

Greece had not participated with combat forces in the 2003 Bush-Blair invasion of Iraq. The anti-war movement in Greece was among the most massive and socially rooted of any in the world. And it had a pronounced internationalist and anti-racist flavour. There was something of a discounting – through taking for granted – of the Greek anti-war movement at the great gatherings against the G8 in Genoa in 2001 and of the European Social Forum (ESF) in Florence a year later. The ESF brought together the manifold forces of the European left and social movements which had either emerged or been rejuvenated following the Seattle protests at the turn of the millennium. They had signalled the birth of a movement against capitalist globalisation and – following 9/11 – imperialist war.

One reason why the scale of the anti-war movement in Greece was considered unexceptional was a deeply rooted public opinion in opposition to Greece's Nato membership and to specifically US aggression and foreign policy. The US state and its adjutant in Britain had intervened decisively in Greece during the civil war and again with the Colonels' coup of 1967 against the left. Terms such as 'US imperialism' were not confined to a socially marginal far left but were part of the language of popular Greece. Neoliberal friends of the government of Costas Simitis in 2001 publicly bemoaned the fact that there were only two countries in the world – Greece and Indonesia – where, on the Saturday following the 9/11 attacks, demonstrations took place directed *at* the US embassy rather than against 'Islamist terrorism'.

The Nato war over Kosovo had taken place two years earlier. The left in Europe was divided over the Blair-Clinton adventure. In part that was because it was presented as a 'humanitarian intervention' by centre-left politicians. Their credibility was untarnished, having just ended a decade and a half of rule by the Tory and Republican right. There was no such division on the left in Greece. There was an enormous anti-war movement. Its principal leadership was in the hands of the Communist Party. One result of that was to encourage a distinctly 'left nationalist' rather than explicitly internationalist tone to the demonstrations. In May 1999, towards the end of the 78-day bombing campaign, I reported from one of the huge protests in Athens. As well as slogans and red banners of the left, there were large numbers of Greek flags. It was nothing like the sea of Greek flags I had witnessed some years earlier while observing, certainly not taking part in, one of the state-sponsored anti-Macedonian demonstrations in 1992. At that time, the Greek political class campaigned with the most ferocious chauvinism against the former Yugoslav republic of Macedonia actually calling itself Macedonia. In contrast, the movement against the Kosovo war had a pronounced left character. But it encompassed an uncomfortable ambiguity. Many leading figures oscillated between political denunciation of US imperialist aggression and communalist expressions of solidarity with 'brother Orthodox' Christian Serbia. While not characterising the mobilisations, that meant that national chauvinist ideas and even political forces of that stripe could coexist alongside universalist, anti-war sentiment on the protests. On the fringes it was possible even for some who held xenophobic ideas about the then recently arrived migrants from the collapse of the Albanian state a few years previously to voice their prejudices in the name of opposing the bombing of Belgrade. It was left to a strand of the internationalist left explicitly to confront such prejudices. That they did so was both to their credit and also bore fruit two years later in the development of the movement against the Afghanistan and Iraq wars.

The mobilisations over Iraq were thoroughly internationalist in flavour. Of course there was no 'imaginary community' of co-religionist or ethnic interest between Orthodox Christian Greeks and majority Muslim Iraqis. But that was not the only reason. There was a conscious and concerted effort on the part of the driving forces behind the movement to make explicit the internationalism which led to the unprecedented global mobilisations of 15 February 2003. I witnessed several anti-war rallies and events throughout 2002 in Greece. At all of them there was a prominent presence of the Pakistani and Arab immigrant communities of Greece, then quite marginal to political life. There was often also either a Turkish speaker – whether from Turkey or from the Turkish minority in Greece – or a message from the sister anti-war movement across the Aegean. There was joyful celebration in the Greek anti-war movement in March of 2003 when its Turkish counterpart was able to have the most direct political effect of the whole anti-war campaign internationally by pressuring the parliament in Ankara to refuse the necessary majority required for the 14 airbases in Turkey to be used to muster a northern front for the imminent war on Iraq. In preventing a two-pronged offensive, that political development had a profound effect on the conduct of the war and consequently upon the enlarged space for the anti-occupation insurgency which developed in central Iraq.

The organising centre of the Greek anti-war movement operated in close cooperation with the British Stop the War Coalition. But the similar priority of making support for the Palestinian national struggle and opposition to Islamophobia central planks of its agitation was not some extra-national imposition on the Greek political reality. While the salience of the 'Muslim question' was seemingly slighter in Greece than in Britain at the outbreak of war, the choice of the core of the movement nonetheless to confront Islamophobia directly arose from an assessment of the likely course of developments. That judgement proved prescient.

The Pasok government of Costas Simitis had strongly aligned itself with the modernising trend of European social democracy for which Tony Blair's New Labour in Britain was the advance guard. Already in 1999 that had meant that, while forced to bend to the overwhelming public opposition to the Kosovo war, Simitis and his foreign minister George Papandreou had tried to bring Greece as close as they dared to the Nato war effort and had resisted, successfully, the opposition to bombing flowing over to forcing Greece to abrogate its treaty commitments. Pasok's room for manoeuvre was curtailed, but the government survived the war on its neighbour without serious loss of autonomy in foreign affairs. A bona fide of being thoroughly modern at the time was taken to be adoption of the supposedly, and speciously, new and 'internationalist' policy of 'humanitarian intervention' and its offspring, the Responsibility to Protect doctrine. Until the full disaster of the Iraq intervention became inescapably obvious in the latter half of the decade, the doctrine of a responsibility to intervene militarily in the name of humanitarianism informed state and non-state bureaucracies, from the US State Department, through parts of the United Nations (UN) and even some international non-governmental organisations (NGOs) and large charities. Despite containing within its ranks a considerable old-style nationalist component and parliamentary cohort, the government of New Democracy's Costas Karamanlis, which came to power in spring 2004 with an unexpected 45 per cent of the vote, shared much of the orientation of the 'New Pasok' administration it replaced.

If 'modernising' military intervention abroad was one pillar of a consensus which united the Blairite centre left with the hard right of George Bush, Spain's recently ousted José María Aznar and Italy's Silvio Berlusconi, then racialised pressure upon Europe's Muslim minority was the counterpart at home. First, it flowed as a necessary concomitant to fighting a series of wars against Muslim majority states – including, by implication, support for what amounts to a colonial extension of Europe, Israel, in its wars against Lebanon and the Palestinian enclave of Gaza. Second, it became an ineluctable ideological refuge for states and political actors who had to face the intransigent reality of widespread opposition among Muslims at home and abroad to Western policy. Proponents of that policy could not entertain even the possibility that such hostility arose from the West's hypocrisies and brutalities, just as decades of US intervention had given rise across Latin America to a similar anti-imperialist sentiment in Catholic-majority nations. Instead, an overarching pathologising of Muslims began to seize every government and security state apparatus across Europe, even in countries such as Greece and France, which had not deployed troops in the Iraq war. In many European states the new transatlantic anti-Muslim racism fused with extant xenophobic and racist ideologies directed against immigrants from Muslim regions. In Greece there was a particular twist. In order to deny that there was any kind of internal question of national minority rights, the Greek state had, since a major national clash with Turkey which almost led to war in the 1950s, referred to the Turkish minority in its northernmost region as 'Muslim'. Now that state-imposed religious identification, far from signalling an enforced assimilation as a nationally indistinct religious minority into majority Orthodox society (there are small Catholic and Protestant minorities in Greece also) served, in the climate of the 'clash of civilisations', to index Muslims as a potential enemy within. The imputation was not now of a divided loyalty between Athens and a secular, irredentist military bureaucracy in Ankara, but of a choice between participation in Western liberal democracy and commitment to the barbarism of Al Qaeda.

The anti-Islamophobic cutting edge of the movement against the Iraq war flowed from a wager on the part of its central organisers that anti-Muslim racism, and in its wake the rehabilitation and refashioning of older racial prejudices, would become a central feature of Greek politics. That did indeed happen in the following decade. The portal of entry for this new racism was not some anti-modern traditionalism in Greek society and expressions of it in varied parts of the political spectrum. It was, in fact, the very driving forces of neoliberal modernisation. The first decisive moment was the decision by the Greek government and state in the summer of 2005 to throw itself into the 'war on terror'. This marked a new and insidious phase of scapegoating politics which, though it originated in a political centre which was itself to become more extreme, predictably found its sharpest manifestation on the right and far right. And that, in turn, also evoked a new, radical anti-racist politics.

One consequence of the positions adopted by the anti-war movement was to increase the space for an 'anti-systemic' internationalism. The caricature of the anti-Kosovo war movement painted by modernising social democratic and liberal opinion was that it was stuck in the past. The mercifully short-lived 'Euston Manifesto' camarilla of liberal imperialist bomberati in London in 2003–4 had its counterparts in parts of the Greek media and political class. The left – which in Greece meant those issuing from the Communist tradition – had undergone a backwards evolution to become small-minded nationalists nostalgic for national sovereignty in an era in which it was being swept away by the forces of globalisation. So ran the argument. Global concern for human rights had apparently transfigured enormously powerful and undemocratic institutions such as the Pentagon and Nato alliance, turning them into bearers of the just society the world over. The arguments of 'left patriotic' elements – the KKE most outstandingly – appeared to confirm in Greece that it was modernisers of the centre, in tactical alliance with the neo-conservatives in the Bush administration, who were the real internationalists, promulgating a reheated version of the liberal imperialism championed by British Prime Minister Gladstone in the last third of the nineteenth century. Fittingly, the Victorian Liberal leader had articulated his doctrine in the course of campaigning for British imperial military intervention in Greece and the Balkans in the 1870s.

The anti-war movement in Greece of this millennium created a narrative in opposition to what was, in essence, a continuation of the grand assertion at the end of the Cold War that the left was dead and that it was liberal capitalism which stood not only without a credible alternative but as the true liberating global force. The whole history of the anti-capitalist left was held to be nothing but a parenthetic, and totalitarian, aberration. The new reality of a mass social movement in which Palestinian flags outnumbered Greek ones, however, encouraged those forces on the left whose opposition to a US-British war drive flowed from a universalist internationalism rather than a Greek exceptionalism. It rejuvenated the left. While the driving force for the movement came from outside of Synaspismos and what was to become Syriza, the radical left electoral coalition was well placed to articulate the new social movement in the political sphere. As would often be the case in the succeeding 10 years, it was not that there was some automatic gain at the ballot box. Rather, what it did was start to cohere patterns of oppositional public opinion – mass consciousness – and the political positions of many activists in what was still a minority movement, though enjoying the support of majority opinion. It was only latterly that these processes translated into a decisive shift of political allegiance electorally and in other ways.

Something else decisive took place in the summer of 2005 in response to the brute state force – Greek, British and Pakistani – deployed against the Muslim Pakistani migrants of Greece. It was the emergence of first the Pakistanis and then other recently arrived migrants as an organised force in Greek society and politics, whatever their status on the electoral roll. Greece had experienced previous patterns of immigration. Largely, however, these had been of people defined as ethnically or linguistically Greek following the end of the First World War and the upheavals when the former Soviet Union collapsed in the early 1990s. The Albanian immigration in the middle of that decade was exceptional in a country which had long been marked by emigration to more developed or rapidly growing capitalist states – West Germany, Australia, the US. National assimilation had characterised public policy regarding the 'lost Greeks' who arrived from the Black Sea area following the Soviet collapse. From its inception the Greek state had been remarkably adept at constructing a single cultural identity from disparate groups of people who were, stage by stage, absorbed into its expanding territory despite vast differences of language, lived culture and even national allegiance. With membership of the EU, then of the Schengen area of free movement in parts of Europe and latterly of the euro currency, Greece for the first time shared the experience of population flows into the more developed northern or core European states – France and Germany – to which, only a generation before, it had been itself a tributary supplier of labour. Modern Greece had not had an empire. But by virtue of its alliances through Nato and the EU it experienced, in the 2000s, something of the British and French post-imperial demographic and social upheaval.

There was a tiny, older and well-established Pakistani community in Greece. But by the middle of the 2000s most of the Pakistani – as well as Bangladeshi, Arab and a variety of African – immigrants were very recent arrivals. And their arrival coincided with the rewind of the film of an ever expansive, welcoming Europe. Its replacement was a hardening security state and associated divisive ideology directed against those within and without who bordered the continent to the east and to the south, across the Mediterranean.

Under the impetus of the radicalisation of the anti-capitalist and anti-war movements in the first half of the decade – and in no small part thanks to the determined efforts of the radical left within them – the result was not some flattening assimilation into a bland, Blairite imaginarium, one where cosmopolitanism equalled the pallid smorgasbord of inedibles on offer to IMF and other functionaries in some Hilton franchise hotel in one world city or another. Instead, Greece's new migrant and refugee communities were to emerge as combative forces in opposition movements to a state which was thoroughly European in its exclusion of the Asian, African and Arab.

It is tempting to take for granted the resistance mounted by Greece's new migrant communities. What certainly cannot be so assumed is the transformative effect that they had on layers of the society and of the political left. In 2006 I attended a meeting of the executive of the powerful Athens Labour Centre, which coordinates several union bodies in the capital. It was addressed by the British-Pakistani anti-war and radical left leader Salma Yaqoob. No Muslim woman wearing a hijab had ever spoken at such a meeting in Greece. She was warmly received. Earlier that year, the national confederation of unions in the private sector, GSEE, had posted the €20,000 bail imposed on Javed Aslam, who faced prosecution and possible deportation for his leadership of the campaign to expose the torture and illegal abduction of his compatriots in Greece at the behest of the British state. Somebody had to organise to make those encounters happen at the interface between the new movements, in which new social subjects – immigrants from the Indian subcontinent, for example – played a prominent role, and the established structures thrown up in generations of earlier struggle. It is to the enormous credit of that section of the Greek left which imaginatively bridged those domains that such a cross-fertilisation took place. The result was little noticed a decade ago. Today it is an unprobed assumption that there are so many Greek young people and activists whose response to the throttling of their country at the hands of the Troika is to see themselves as of a piece with Muslim women in Tahrir Square or Palestinian fighters in Gaza.

That assessment of the battle in Greece as an aspect of a wider war rather than as an essentially Greek struggle is not universal. But, even to the extent that it is held by a section of the left in Greece today, it came to depend on a succession of confrontations – always starting with a minority which appeared unfashionably intransigent in its slogans – with a vicious and powerful racist offensive. The monster of racist and scapegoating ideology, once born in the union of corporate globalisation and military aggression, did not stay within the confines of securocrats and technocrats. With traditional political allegiances and just-so stories of the mainstream shattered by the severity of the crisis swallowing Greece in the latter half of the 2000s, such themes became the tools of those who sought to shore up the old order. It did not start with the pseudo-populist fascist right. Nor even with the bigots of the national conservative Tories, as represented within New Democracy by Samaras. The first toxic deployment of racism for naked political ambition came from the ranks of Pasok.

Operation Broom

On taking office in October 2009 Pasok immediately revealed that the state of the public finances was far worse than the previous government had let on. Nevertheless, it exuded in its first few months an air of business as usual. The severity of the economic crisis shattered that illusion by spring of the following year. As Papandreou turned to the international institutions which would become known as the Troika to secure a financial bailout, he was confronted by the first enormous wave of opposition to austerity policies which were to savage the country.

A generation earlier, the Pasok government of George Papandreou's father, Andreas, had also found itself facing financial and economic crisis, and had turned to austerity. Hopes for a more equal distribution of wealth evaporated. Nevertheless, Andreas had managed to push through some enduring liberalising social reforms, such as divorce and breaking the church's monopoly on marriage. The explicitly free market, modernising government of Costas Simitis at the turn of the millennium had found the political reserves to face down right-wing nationalist reaction and to remove from Greek identity cards the requirement to state the bearer's religion. Modern social democracy might have given up on anything resembling socialist economic policies but could be relied upon to defend and extend individual rights in the social sphere. At least that was Pasok's thin promise as the economy went into free fall. It managed to pass in 2010 a very modest measure to provide a route to citizenship for some children of the increasing number of immigrants who lacked that status. The 'Ragoussis Law' did nothing for the children of more recent arrivals – Pakistani, Arab, African – but did at least do something to allow the legal integration of Albanian children, a lot of whom by then were high school students. That in itself was refutation of the racist scaremongering of the 1990s that they and their parents would never fit in to Greek society. That limited measure was to turn out to be the only decision by the Pasok government which could be regarded as remotely progressive. And even that was overshadowed by its resort to a rhetoric which became increasingly illiberal as it both imposed deeply unpopular austerity measures and competed with a right-wing opposition New Democracy party which turned to xenophobic populism.

Samaras won the leadership of the New Democracy opposition party following its 2009 general election defeat. He combined an opportunist anti-memorandum line with a sharp turn to national conservative themes. The tensions within New Democracy exploded in May 2010 when there was a small split. Samaras was in no position to assail the government from the left and had no intention of doing so. Rather, his temporary anti-memorandum line served to secure a position from which to articulate the hard right, national chauvinist politics which, two decades before, had seen him split from New Democracy to set up his own short-lived national populist party. As Samaras consolidated public support throughout 2010, the strand within Pasok which had always been more patriotic than left wing began to look to how it might survive the deepening unpopularity of the government. In the summer of 2011, the minister for 'health and social solidarity', Andreas Loverdos, played his card. He chose a gathering at the UN in New York to begin a political campaign which has never been surpassed in the history of treachery on the social democratic left against supposedly inviolable principles.

On 9 June 2011 Loverdos told the UN meeting of health experts that Greece faced a crisis over rising HIV and AIDS infection. The collapse of primary health care, HIV services, and safer sex and clean needles programmes were indeed leading to a crisis, as friends told me on the Athens Pride demonstration that summer. The maverick right-wing Pasok minister, however, adduced other reasons for the epidemic. It was, he told the gathering, due to the influx into Greece of illegal immigrants from Africa and Eastern Europe. HIV transmission from these aliens into the healthy body of Greek society was, he maintained, via immigrant prostitutes infecting presumably decent Greek male clients. Among those who were shocked by the baseless claim – made with every word accented towards misogyny and racism – were Greek health experts from the ministry and from NGOs. When challenged about his evidence base by them afterwards, Loverdos said, 'I have my own sources.' There turned out to be no such sources. But that did not stop him in the following months doggedly developing the Goebbels-like narrative.

Papandreou's government collapsed in November 2011, but Loverdos survived as health minister in the coalition administration which succeeded it, headed by the impeccably pro-EU, technocratic – and never elected – banker, Lucas Papademos. With elections imminent and Pasok in what would prove to be a terminal crisis, the minister for social solidarity gave practical and material effect to his speech a few months before. Together with public order minister Mihalis Chrisochoidis he launched in early 2012 what the press dubbed a 'sweeping operation' (literally 'operation broom' in Greek). It was a cleansing sweep in central Athens. The detritus to be cleaned off the streets were dozens of women held to be the alien prostitutes who were infecting the salubrious Greek family man. The deluge in the millionaire-owned media, print and broadcast, was nearly overwhelming. Night after night they carried the pictures, names and nationalities of desperate women rounded up by the robocops of the Greek security state. As the Papademos government achieved what Papandreou had bridled at, imposing a second, even more devastating austerity memorandum (now with the participation of New Democracy and the far right LAOS party in an unholy alliance with Pasok), Loverdos and his friends took to the television studios to fan a carefully crafted and utterly cynical racist panic.

The one-time centrist pretender to the leadership of his party led the way in attempting to outflank the worst political forces of the right. The supposed moderniser used an obscure edict from 1940 as the legal base for the witch-hunt. It was painstakingly orchestrated, playing on misogyny – calculating women infecting decent men; racism – the prostitutes were foreigners; and traditional anti-Communism – some of the women were from Bulgaria, which was held up in the far right's imagination as an eternal enemy of Greece thanks to the Balkan wars of a century before and because Bulgaria gave refuge to Communist fighters following their defeat in the civil war of the 1940s. Not a particle of this narrative was true.

Dozens of women were forcibly tested for HIV. Some 32 tested positive. They were charged with 'conspiracy to commit grievous bodily harm'. Months later – and following the general elections of May and June – the charges were quietly shelved in almost all cases. As is so often the case with such scare stories, the gory headlines about 'Killer Prossies' and 'Migrant Whores' at the height of a panic induced from above gave way, in the cold light of facts, to short paragraphs buried on unread pages reporting that the vast majority of the women herded into police cells and subject to the forced insertion of intravenous needles were in fact Greek. Most of them were not sex workers.

The great lie, however, had achieved the status of urban legend. And despite Pasok's collapse in the general elections, Loverdos and his collaborators were returned to a parliament now dominated by New Democracy, but with Syriza replacing Pasok as the second party. In the May and June elections all three parties of the outgoing grand coalition lost support. LAOS fell below the 3 per cent threshold and was out of the parliament. But with 7.5 and 6.9 per cent respectively, the national chauvinists of ANEL and the fascists of Golden Dawn secured parliamentary representation. With 29.7 per cent of the vote, New Democracy headed a coalition including Pasok, with 12 per cent, and on 6.3 per cent the centre-left Dimar, a breakaway to its right from Syriza, which was the official opposition with 26.9 per cent. The success of the right-wing nationalists and fascists was not lost on Samaras. His government swiftly executed a sharp turn to overt racist policy, deepening the furrow already tilled by Pasok's Loverdos.

Operation 'Hospitable Zeus'

In the run-up to the elections, Samaras had already signalled the course he was to follow as prime minster. In April, he said, 'Greece today has become a centre for illegal immigrants. We must take back our cities where the illegal trade in drugs, prostitution, counterfeit goods is booming. There are many diseases, and I am not only talking about Athens but elsewhere too.'[18] That summer the right-wing media was awash with anti-immigrant stories. In the depression-hit centre of Athens and other major Greek cities, the new migrant communities were a visible presence. Their concentration in the run-down streets south of the city centre appeared to confirm the claim that it was their arrival within Greek society which was in some way responsible for the national economic disaster. Already, 12 months earlier in May 2011, there had been nothing short of a three-day pogrom in the streets south of Omonoia Square and in other areas. In the course of the racist violence, which lawyers acting for the Jail Golden Dawn initiative were later to demonstrate was orchestrated by leading figures of the fascist party, 21-year-old migrant Bangladeshi worker Alim Abdul Manan was murdered and scores seriously wounded. He was not to be the last.

Incoming interior minister Nikos Dendias took up where Loverdos had left off. Where Loverdos had claimed that foreign sex workers constituted a 'health bomb', Dendias said that immigration was 'a bomb aimed at the foundations of society and of the state'. He and the government rapidly moved from rhetoric to action with the full force of the state. He announced 'Operation Xenios Zeus'. 'Xenios' was one of the appellations in Greek mythology of the god Zeus, meaning 'hospitable' or 'he who looks after strangers'. Not only was the name given to this policy of rounding up immigrants beyond Orwellian in its double-speak, the date chosen to announce it could not have indicated more clearly the abandonment of liberal democratic norms by a government, which, lest it be forgotten, included self-declared defenders of human rights, the centre-left parties Pasok and Dimar.

The round-up of thousands of immigrants began on 4 August, the date on which, in 1936, General Ioannis Metaxas had seized power in a fascistic coup, ousting the elected liberal government. The significance of the date could not be missed. The right-wing elements which dominate the Athens police force certainly took it as a signal for a display of brutality above and beyond their usual standards. While ostensibly aimed at 'undocumented migrants' the repression, of course, fell upon all who 'looked foreign', Africans, Arabs and Asians. Arriving in Athens that August, friends cautioned me that years of familiarity with the city's streets and with Greek culture would count for nothing if I, fairly dark-skinned, was foolish enough to leave my British passport at home and was to run into one of the packs of heavily armoured policemen who would appear out of nowhere on street corners and set up what felt like the checkpoints of an occupying power.

The cash-strapped Greek government readily found the funds to open a gulag archipelago of 'hospitality centres' to incarcerate those seized from the street. Within a year, the numbers passing through these black prisons – largely beyond independent oversight – reached an estimated 20,000. No one knows for sure. But the numbers were probably double Greece's regular prison population, and the conditions of their detention were even worse. In December 2012, the UN special rapporteur on migrants' human rights, François Crépeau, told reporters after visiting various camps:

In general, the detainees had little or no information about why they were detained, and how long they would remain in detention. This also applied to some of those who had engaged lawyers, and they complained that the lawyers simply take their money and do not follow up on their cases. Those who had applied for asylum often had no information about the status of their case, and others had not been able to apply for asylum from the detention facility. The medical services offered in some of the facilities by the Hellenic Centre for Disease Control and Prevention were highly insufficient. Most of the detention facilities I visited lacked heating and hot water, and the detainees complained about insufficient amounts and poor quality of food, lack of soap and other hygiene products, as well as insufficient clothing and blankets.[19]

Throughout early August, Dendias relished his role as 'hard man' of the government. The street-fighting hard men of Golden Dawn took their cue from the police. Anti-racist groups sounded the alarm at rising levels of serious racist assault. On holiday on the Pelion peninsula with friends, we did our best both to relax and also maintain some political optimism. There was little or none to be gained from the papers or television channels. With Pasok a part of a coalition government which could be more accurately described as hard right rather than centre right, and with Syriza regarded by many news organisations as barely legitimate, there was scarcely any voice reported in opposition to the racist and authoritarian offensive. We headed back early to Athens to join dutifully a protest demonstration on the last weekend of August. Arriving from Larissa bus station a little late to Omonoia Square we anticipated a small but determined gathering, already consoling ourselves with the line that 'you have to start somewhere'. Instead, what we found ourselves part of was something extraordinary – and a sign of things to come.

With so many new migrants – at least half – lacking legal papers, the authorities, and just about everybody else, had assumed that they would vacate all public space and go into hiding to escape the round-ups. Omonoia Square and the streets radiating from it were, however, packed that day with many thousands of immigrants – the largest number from the Pakistani community who had suffered the 'disappearances' in the wake of the London bombings seven years before. There were probably 15,000 people. That was pretty big for any political, as opposed to trade union, demonstration in Athens, even by the measure of the previous two years of agitation against austerity. What was unique was its composition. Barring a tiny percentage comprising the part of the Greek left which had been particularly alert to the dangers of racism and fascism and which had launched the KEERFA coalition to oppose Golden Dawn in 2009, the demonstrators were wholly of the often undocumented new migrant communities. Far from being driven out of the public space, the demonstration – which combined defiant resistance to the round-up with fearless opposition to Golden Dawn – showed that the Pakistanis and other recent arrivals were opening up a fresh front of social struggle against the government. Furthermore, its political orientation was explicitly towards the left, however thin on the ground the actual Greek left was that day. The seeds sown nearly a decade earlier by the internationalist anti-war movement had germinated – and had been nurtured carefully by the forces which had planted them. So among the speakers, who were lightly sprinkled between music, chanting and marching (which was a forceful affair from which the Athens police wisely kept their distance), were Javed Aslam from the Pakistani community and Petros Constantinou, one of the public faces of the movement against the Iraq war in 2003 and the national coordinator of KEERFA.

Not for the last time, speeches and slogans from the migrant minority went out of their way to assail the austerity policies of the government and of the EU as jointly responsible with the racism of the state and of Golden Dawn for the murderous treatment they were protesting against. Embracing warmly and scarcely able to hear one another amid chants of 'God is great! Smash the fascists and the memorandum-mongers!' Javed Aslam explained to me:

There are European politicians attacking the Greeks for the police brutality and the rise of Golden Dawn. The police are brutal. Golden Dawn are fascists. There is racism in Greece. But this is not because the Greeks are not hospitable. This is the policy of a government that the EU support. This is because of the austerity, which is hurting Greeks and non-Greeks. I wish more Greeks were here. And then they would see that we are not the problem. We are lions roaring against the same government that is oppressing them. But whoever else is here, we will continue to be here.

Those words signposted the direction for what was to become a militant part of the social resistance over the next two and half years – a resistance which was eventually to bring down Samaras's government. The impact of the migrants' movement on politics and on the left was not through delivering electoral support to Syriza. Most of those on the streets on that marvellous day in late August 2012 could not vote. On the narrowest of electoral calculations there appeared to be more to be won by not being seen to be 'soft on immigration' than in taking part in such demonstrations. At best, the diffusion of anti-racist arguments helped to blunt the electoral impact of racist politics, if that was the terrain under consideration. But the effect was much more pronounced upon the other movements of opposition to austerity and the government. First, it established a gulf between the migrant communities alongside the, often young, anti-racists who rallied to their support and those pro-EU NGOs and organisations which tried in vain to convince young, cosmopolitan Greece that their ideals were shared by allegedly liberal European institutions in Brussels. The militancy and left-wing character of the migrant struggle proved an obstacle to later attempts to co-opt it under the wing of liberal, free market forces.

Second, the radicalised immigrant communities proved true to their slogans of seeking a common front with working-class Greece in the central battles against austerity. That meant there was a visible presence of Pakistani and of other more recent arrivals in all sorts of struggles throughout 2013 and 2014 – from the battle by workers at the state broadcaster ERT against its closure to the struggle by the 595 women cleaners of the finance ministry against mass sacking, and including also the heroic struggle by the Bangladeshi strawberry pickers in Manolada, who were shot by their foremen for going on strike in April 2013 over unpaid wages. Migrant participation in those struggles brought to the surface and made explicit arguments directly confronting the anti-immigrant and Islamophobic scapegoating which the government, and in its slipstream Golden Dawn, continued to pump out up to its crushing defeat at the polls in January 2015. Before that victory for the left, however, the path deeper into the maze of the austerity memorandums, authoritarianism and violent racism was to take further, dangerous twists. At each, the grunts of Golden Dawn grew louder. The monster's appetite was to claim more victims. And then it lurked, waiting for the new government of the left to lose its way.

CHAPTER FIVE

Lost in the Labyrinth

The hopes of January 2015 remained high as the government embarked on negotiations with the Troika in February. The international coverage was marked by a combination of hostility and disbelief at the anti-austerity line of the new government on the one hand, and trivialisation of it on the other. The dress-down, tie-less style of Tsipras and his ministers became the symbol for the mass media both to indicate the novelty of the Syriza government and simultaneously to embark on a long battle aimed at neutering it into merely a sartorial variant of a politics which admitted of no systemic alternative. The fashion sense of finance minister Yanis Varoufakis received acres of coverage in a celebrity-obsessed media. His appearance in a photo shoot in *Paris Match*, which he later said he regretted, had a contradictory impact. It showed that the new government enjoyed far from pariah status among the European public. But it also provided an image for the right to resurrect months later in its attempts to scapegoat Varoufakis personally for the economic strangulation the eurozone inflicted on Greece.

A more substantial indicator of a breach with the old politics came on the streets of Athens. In response to a call on Facebook, thousands of people – beyond the ranks of Syriza activists and not called out officially by the party – rallied in Syntagma Square outside the parliament on the evening of 5 February. Countless demonstrations had filled the square in the crisis years. This one, uniquely however, was in support of the government and its combative stance against the Troika's demands for austerity and business as usual. The support was heartfelt, but not without independence of mind and spirit. An unemployed health worker, Maria Manouli, who was there with her children, voiced the sentiment of many:

I want Mr Varoufakis to tell the bloodsuckers what they can do with their memorandum. I hope they are watching now. I'm here to tell them that it is not just our finance minister they are up against. The people of Greece are behind him. That's what the election showed. I like Alexis [Tsipras]. I used to vote for Pasok, but not any more. I'm not one of the young people who got this protest going – and I'm really glad they did. I remember lots of governments, and I know how serious the situation is. So I am here now to help make things clear. We want this government because we want jobs and a future. There's lots of media here so I am sure the prime minister will see this. We're with you, Alexis. Don't let us down.[20]

Support for the government extended beyond those who had voted for it or for the left. New Democracy had fought a scaremongering campaign. Pasok had echoed the right-wing line that a Syriza government would immediately find itself isolated and that Greece would rapidly become the Gaza Strip of Europe, its government treated by international powers as pariahs. Instead, there was, despite the trivialisation, considerable comment in the global media about how Greece's new government was a breath of fresh air, despite its presumed eccentric ideas. That was testament to the deep public antipathy in Europe to the old political establishment and sympathy for anything new. In retrospect, certainly, it was also a sign of the long game the European elites had settled on after coming to terms even before the election with the fact that their political allies on the centre right and centre left in Greece were not only going to be turfed out, but that they had also, in the manner of a middle-ranking City trader sending rose-tinted reports to his boss, concealed the full extent of the crisis they were in. The whirlwind of media coverage – perversely even the *Paris Match* feature – and meetings with European counterparts were not lost on millions of working-class and impoverished Greeks. Their political yardsticks are somewhat plainer than those of professional commentators, and therefore frequently yield greater insight. Whether on radio phone-ins, from taxi drivers or looking for bargains in street markets you could, in the first month of the Syriza government, hear a variant of the same refrain from that mass of people who go out of their way to say they are 'not political': 'Well – they lied didn't they. Again. They said that everyone would turn on us. But everyone wants to talk to Alexis. He's doing ok.'

The opinion polls in mid February suggested that if an election were called the following Sunday Syriza would win not the 36 per cent it got on 25 January, but around 50 per cent of the vote. The old parties of government were in crisis. Syriza had the active support of a minority, prepared under its own initiative to call sizeable protests on the side of the government. It enjoyed great sympathy among the less engaged, but very large, middle ground. There could scarcely be more favourable circumstances for a government committed to a strategy of robust negotiation with the Troika to end the social disaster of austerity.

All the more shocking, then, was the deal the government signed in Brussels on 20 February. So great was the goodwill on the left in Greece and internationally that many felt inhibited in criticising the agreement to extend the strictures of the hated austerity memorandums for four months. Some claimed at first that it had 'bought time' in which, presumably, the extraordinarily favourable political conditions of February might in some way be bettered. The anti-capitalist Antarsya coalition outside of Syriza issued a statement opposing the deal. The Communist Party denounced it, but like the boy who cried wolf this message fell on many a deaf ear since it denounced everything. A turning point came with an intervention which could not be pigeon-holed as 'Well they would say that, wouldn't they?'

Syriza MEP Manolis Glezos's voice could in no way be discounted. Days into the Nazi occupation of Greece he had climbed the iconic Acropolis in Athens on 30 May 1941 to tear down the Swastika and replace it with the Greek flag. He went on to fight in the war of liberation and then with the left in the civil war. Arrests, torture, escapes – and the distinction of being sentenced to death multiple times by German Nazism, Italian fascism and the Greek monarchist right – were combined with a second kind of courage: to stay steadfastly loyal to the left but to speak openly when he felt it was wrong. Within 36 hours, Glezos issued a statement via the anti-austerity organisation he had founded, flatly opposing the deal as an unnecessary retreat. In words echoing black radical Malcolm X and before him Irish revolutionary Padraig Pearce, 92-year-old Glezos said, 'There can be no compromise between the oppressor and oppressed. Between the slave and the occupier. The only solution is freedom.'

Others swiftly raised their voices. Newly elected Syriza MP and renowned Marxist economist Costas Lapavitsas posed five questions about the deal. They demonstrated it was incompatible both with the pledge to end the humiliating nightmare of the memorandum years and with the 'Thessaloniki Programme' to alleviate social suffering in Greece, on which Syriza had won the election. Detailed analysis of the deal is now redundant. Not only was it overtaken by events but, within two months, first economics minister Euclid Tsakalotos[21] and then the prime minister himself accepted that it had been a mistake. But the damage had been done. First, the government had claimed in February that what it later acknowledged was a bad deal and mistake was actually a 'victory'. That risked fanning cynicism – this lot is as untrustworthy as the old lot. However unfair that charge, the government's conventional spin doctoring – one of the reasons cited most frequently across the European public for its mistrust of all politicians – opened the door and invited it in. Second, the huge problem with the deal was not in its detailed concessions; within days it proved to be short of the itemised austerity measures demanded by the Troika in any case. It was that it locked the government in Athens into a process of months of negotiations in which, far from buying time, the financial and economic levers the agreement had left in the hands of the Troika meant that Syriza's negotiating position was progressively weakened. Third, by restating that he would take 'no unilateral action' regarding defaulting on the unpayable debt or in other ways conflicting with membership of the euro, Tsipras was saying the government would not yank back any of those levers by, for example, shifting the economic burden onto Greek capitalists through nationalising the banking system and seizing wealth which would otherwise flee the country. The result was to place the Greek government in a position similar to those who find themselves at the mercy of payday loan companies.

Dangled on the thread of debt

There was still €7.2 billion outstanding from the second memorandum bailout, which was coming to an end. The memorandums copper-fastened a permanent pressure on any government in Athens to impose a radical restructuring of the economy in the interests of corporate power. That is the rationale of austerity. Tranches of bailout would be released only after Greece passed periodic reviews to see how well it had done in implementing measures which went way beyond cutting public spending. It was as if you were on a permanent performance review by your manager and paid three months in arrears. The measures were fundamentally about removing 'rigidities' in the labour market and welfare system – that is destroying those legal, trade union and other protections of working people against corporate greed which were still intact, thanks to the extraordinary levels of social resistance in Greece. There was much talk of loss of sovereignty arising from this mechanism binding Greece to the demands of foreign creditors. But, whose sovereignty? As explained in chapter 3, the Greek business class was fully signed up to the policy of their European counterparts. There was no loss of sovereign power for them. Quite the opposite. They saw in the memorandums a means to force the government and agencies of state to do what they had failed to do for decades, despite the Thatcher-Blair rhetoric of modernisation: break working-class resistance to free market capitalism, still sedimented in employment regulation, trade union organisation, and patterns of expectation and thinking among millions of people. The promise of 'no unilateral action' against the lenders abroad flowed out of a parallel pledge to the business class at home. So, despite holding a big stake in the Greek banking system the government signalled it would not exercise that power, still less move to take over the banks, even though the mechanism for doing so was straightforward.[22] Instead, and with great ingenuity, Syriza's eminently able economics team, led by finance minister Varoufakis, tried to plot a path within the conventional choices. But the Troika was in charge of the rules. And it cut off one escape route after another.

First, it soon became clear that the €7.2 billion outstanding to Greece would not be released until it signed up to a third memorandum. Second, the ECB imposed severe limits on the Greek government issuing what are called Treasury Bills. These are short-term IOUs. All governments use them to cover cash flow shortfalls with a promise to pay back the money in a month to six months' time. Third, it stopped Greek banks from lending to the government by taking on those IOUs. This closed off a temporary lifeline which Varoufakis and other economists had mooted in the election campaign and which the ECB had turned a blind eye to in other cases, when it suited them. The planned escape route was this.

One of the European mechanisms developed to save the continent's banking system, whose reckless lending was exposed by the crisis, was called Emergency Liquidity Assistance (ELA). It is analogous to an overdraft facility as opposed to a long-term loan. Under the ELA the Greek central bank could, only with the approval of the ECB, borrow money from European funds on a short-term basis to pump into the domestic banking system to cover cash flow problems. The ELA rules banned a national central bank from using the funds for anything other than keeping the private banks going. It was explicitly prevented from using them to keep government functions afloat –

such as a health service, state pension pay-outs, paying the public sector wage bill and so on. In banning the Greek banks from lending to the government via buying up its IOUs, the ECB closed a potential indirect mechanism whereby the money from the ELA might have alleviated the budget crisis and actually gone into the ailing Greek economy. Instead, what happened was that the national bank, and therefore ultimately the Greek taxpayer, became liable for the billions pumped in to the private banking system and kept in private hands. From December to mid May 2015, some €35 billion was withdrawn from Greek deposits and the ELA assistance had reached about €80 billion. The Greek national bank had had to offer up collateral to secure that. The ECB would not accept collateral from the private banks as it was deemed worthless. So the national bank had to offer up 'good collateral' – that is a claim on public assets and future state revenues – while getting from the private sector their worthless bits of paper. This was exactly the logic of the global bailouts following the collapse of Lehman Brothers. They had turned a corporate debt crisis into a series of national ones.

Worse, the ELA handed a further weapon to the Troika in its aggressive negotiating strategy. Decisions on increasing the overdraft facility, or calling it in, were taken every Wednesday by the directors of the ECB. Those directors are politically appointed by the 19 governments in the eurozone. They also had the power, at any point, to decree that the collateral offered had declined in value and that either the short-term lending would be cut accordingly or the collateral would have to increase. In other words, by refusing to take the banks out of private control or to take any other 'unilateral action', the government had handed over to the Troika the revolver that would be held to the Greek representatives' heads over five months of negotiations.

Far from buying time, this meant political time running in favour of the Troika and the private sector interests, including the governor of the Greek national bank, who were utterly opposed to bank nationalisation and to any other measure which would hurt them by alleviating the austerity straitjacket. With monthly loan repayments to the IMF rising towards a peak in August, the government was forced to take increasingly desperate measures. The economic impact was to suck money out of the Greek economy, which tipped into recession. Politically, it stored up great problems for the government and provided opportunities for those who sought the defeat of the left.

The parliament passed an emergency measure in May to sequester cash balances held by local government, public corporations and other state bodies. The cash was placed in a Common Fund under the supervision of the Greek central bank and its governor Yannis Stournaras. He was a hangover from the memorandum years. He had been finance minister under Samaras and was fully committed to austerity. Presenting his annual report in February, he directly intervened for the continuation of the status quo and against the policy of a government which had just been elected:

> In the past few years, we have covered some very rough ground at high cost to the whole of Greek society. If we can address the relatively few issues still pending and complete the first phase of the effort launched in 2010, we will then be able to move on to the next phase, in which the growth potential of the economy will be considerably enhanced.[23]

The prefecture of Athens, under Rena Dourou, a close colleague of Tsipras's since their time in the Synaspismos youth in the 1990s, had not waited for a parliamentary edict to hand over €80 million in March. In the stormy council meeting Antarsya representative Dimitra Koutsoumba opposed the move and said, 'You just want to take our money and hand it over to the International Monetary Fund.' That turned out to be close to the truth.

To meet the debt repayments the government took to delaying paying its bills in the health and other sectors. The backlog of unpaid wages and depleted social budgets grew. April provided a glimpse of how perilous the position was and how quickly the popular mood might turn. The payment of state pensions into bank accounts that month was delayed by eight hours. As pensioners queued that morning at the banks only to find that the money was not yet there the news spread through channels as rapid as any fibre optic cable. A friend quipped that those overly in awe of the communications revolution of the internet age have no idea of the capacity of offline, retired Greece to transmit in an instant news from one end of the country to the other and into the most remote village. There was relief when the money reached accounts late that afternoon. But no one was reassured by the unconvincing claim from the government that the delay had been due to a technical hitch. With money already flooding out of the banking system, the 'hitch' was a frightening portent of what a full-blown bank run could look like. The decision the following month to pay €750 million to the IMF a day early compounded the unease that the government was abandoning its priorities. The bulk of that payment came through the one-off trick of drawing down the €650 million Greece was obliged, as a member of the IMF, to deposit in a Washington holding account. In effect, it took out a short-term – with interest – IMF loan to meet a repayment on a longer-term one. The *Financial Times* later revealed that Tsipras had forewarned Germany's Angela Merkel that Greece was on the brink of defaulting on the payment when someone hit upon the idea of raiding the holding account. 'So the German chancellor got a heads up, but my grandmother was left panic-stricken for a day,' as one loyal Syriza student activist bitterly summed up the episode to me.

The decision to raid every public cash reserve and to pay the IMF also created a space for otherwise becalmed and largely discredited political forces to try to rehabilitate themselves and recoup more of a social base. Due to the rhythm of the local government election cycle and its electoral system, most of the municipalities and prefectures were still under the control of Pasok and New Democracy. Mayors of the old order were quick to take to the airwaves claiming that they would resist handing council cash to the central government. That their parties had placed Greece in the maw of the Troika, did not stop them shamelessly posing as opponents of the IMF and blaming the ongoing decline of local government services on Syriza. The government could have slammed the door on any threat of a populist street reaction simply by saying, unequivocally, that the money would not go to the IMF but into paying wages and other public spending. It did not.

The sincerely made promise of the government at the end of February was that it would seek a way out for the country in ongoing negotiations while domestically pressing ahead with a series of reforms, including the central policy of a bill to relieve the humanitarian crisis in the country. The political logic, however, did not lend itself to a neat division between a foreign debt negotiation and a domestic redistribution of wealth and progressive reform. The principal reason is that the debt mechanism was not strictly analogous to a foreign occupation, which was a common image invoked by the anti-memorandum right in ANEL as well as sections of the left. It was an aspect of the internal confrontation within Greece between the working class and poor and the business class, whose interests were served by the nationalisation of the debts they had run up and then the resulting crisis of the state budget becoming the instrument for forcing through neoliberal measures more thoroughly than before.

When it came, the humanitarian crisis bill contained just a tenth of the relief promised in the election campaign. In some ways worse, throughout the month of March the government seemed becalmed and lacking in direction. There was legislative inertia. Though it recovered, the government lost vital time and some sense of cohesion and purpose. Two areas stand out.

Reparations and anti-Germanism

On 10 March Tsipras made a major speech in parliament in the debate to set up a commission to examine the incendiary issue of German war reparations to Greece. The issue was not resolved upon the unification of the German state in 1990 and had been raised under Pasok. There was an extant legal case. It had been judged in the highest court in Greece, granting restitution to the victims of a particularly grizzly massacre by the Waffen SS in the village of Distomo.

A morass of actions, claim and counter-claim surrounded the case involving Italy, Germany and Greece in the international courts and tribunals. But domestically, the Greek courts had given a ruling in favour of the victims. This allowed for the seizure of German state property in Greece to the value set in the judgment. Greek law preferred on the Athens government the right to exercise that seizure or not, as it directly involves relations with other states. The Distomo case was but an aspect of the savagery of the occupation, which had included the Nazi seizure of Greece's wartime bullion reserves and of any moveable property it could lay its hands on.

It was under the conditions of the Cold War that Greece in 1953 was obliged to forego reparations, as the London debt conference wrote off much of the then West German state's liabilities. The creation of a unified Germany in 1990 gave rise to a new legal state entity. The current German state and government, despite the arguments of distinguished German legal experts among others, hides behind the argument that the discontinuities between it and the Third Reich, combined with the 1953 conference, mean that it bears no liability to Greece.

Tsipras's parliamentary speech cogently refuted the moral and legal validity of that evasion. Indeed, it is in its history of military defeat as an imperialist power that Germany throughout the twentieth century attained the status of one of the greatest defaulters on national debt ever, as the liabilities were serially written off for one collapsed German state entity after another. In raising the issue in the run-up to the 70th anniversary of VE Day, commemorated by Syriza government representatives in Moscow, the Greek government was bringing to light the dirty secrets of the Cold War, just at the time when a Cold War era rhetoric was being deployed by the EU and US towards Russia over the intractable crisis in Ukraine.

In that escalating confrontation, German capitalism, while the leading economic force in Europe, was a node in wider alliances. Its allies had their own culpabilities: France for the massacre of Algerian protesters in Paris on 17 October 1961 – when scores of Arab corpses floated down the river of a European capital city without even public perturbation; Britain, with its treachery towards the Greek partisans who had liberated the country from the Nazis.

The reparations question could have provided a point of entry for raising across Europe an alternative to the Cold War narrative and to the pieties of contemporary EU corporate capitalism. That, as well as a morally charged weapon to deploy in the fight to lift austerity from Greece and from the whole of the continent. Instead, and despite a brief verbal fusillade between Berlin and Athens, it turned out to be an elephant which gave birth to a mouse. It gave rise to no action – legal, diplomatic or agitational. All that resulted was a parliamentary committee. It was as if the issue had been disinterred only then to be held up as a holy relic, just as in May the remains of St Barbara were dug up and taken to a cancer hospital in Athens – the power of faith perhaps intended to make up for the lack of chemotherapy and other treatment.

Admittedly, it would have required skill and vigilance to prevent a popular campaign over reparations from descending into a chauvinist anti-German fervour, something I described at the time, paraphrasing the great German socialist August Bebel, as 'the anti-austerity politics of fools'. But in April, 20,000 mainly German demonstrators protested at the opening of the opulent new ECB headquarters in Frankfurt, at a cost to the European public of over €1 billion. Central to their slogans was solidarity with Greece. A month later, rail workers and primary school teachers in Germany struck with wage demands which were most beneficial to the lower paid. There was a path to deployment of the reparations question which was internationalist, anti-fascist and for a radical break with the hypocrisies of European capitalism. And that was in tune with Greek popular opinion. A remarkable feature of the many demonstrations in Greece over the first seven months of 2015 was the absence of anti-German placards, slogans or sentiment. By early summer, however, all that remained from the sound and fury over the reparations issue of March were some government videos shown on the Athens Metro vaguely making the case, a parliamentary committee, which took the issue into the long grass, and some fillip for the nationalist Independent Greeks, who were perfectly happy with Greece being subordinate to the US through Nato, just not to Germany.

Delegitimising Golden Dawn

The passing of the government's humanitarian relief bill was marred by an incident arising from the conduct of the parliamentary vote. Under the Greek constitution and parliamentary procedures 15 MPs may request a roll-call vote – similar to a division in the British parliament. There were 17 Golden Dawn MPs elected in January. All 17 signed a motion to the speaker of the parliament, Zoe Konstantopoulou, for a roll-call vote. Three of the 17, however, remained in prison. And all faced a trial beginning on 20 April for directing a criminal organisation. The trial of Golden Dawn was the fruit of the huge anti-fascist outpouring following the murder of rapper Pavlos Fyssas in September 2013. That eruption, and the ongoing anti-fascist movement, had forced both the media and the Samaras government to break from indulging the fascists as a party just like any other and to throw a *cordon sanitaire* around them. That was a major gain of the movement and, with the fascists waiting in the wings for Syriza to fail, a vital defensive action against them placing themselves at the head of any embittered reaction.

When it came to the vote, Konstantopoulou referred to the petition for a roll-call and asked – as is the procedure – for those requesting it to make their presence known. The constitution is explicit – at least 15 MPs making the request must be present for it to succeed. The judicial authorities had not seen fit to release the three fascist MPs. So 14 fascists took to their feet for their obviously pre-arranged stunt. Instead of saying that the procedural move fell due to lack of 15 presenting MPs, Konstantopoulou said, 'It is true that you are one short, but under the circumstances I am going to use my power of initiative as the speaker to call a roll-call vote myself.'

There was uproar. First on their feet were Communist MPs followed by others. Eventually Nikos Philis, Syriza's chief whip and editor of the party paper *Avgi*, intervened and put considerable distance between himself and the speaker.

It was enough to bring an adjournment in which Konstantopoulou met government ministers and was – parliamentary rumour has it – told by prime minister Alexis Tsipras to back down. She did.

Konstantopoulou was an erratic maverick – certainly no racist. Indeed, a couple of weeks later, on hearing that there was a delegation of trade unionists and Bangladeshi independent, left-wing councillors from London's East End, she invited them to meet her at the parliament, a warm and extraordinarily high-ranking official reception by the third most powerful politician in Greece, according to its constitution. But the Nazis predictably exploited the incident in an effort to rehabilitate themselves on the eve of the trial. Later, when divisions opened within Syriza over the July deal struck with the Troika, Konstantopoulou spoke directly against Golden Dawn in parliament in her speech rejecting a third memorandum. But her earlier procedural indulgence of them was, unfortunately, not a one-off. The foreign minister went on to invite Golden Dawn onto a parliamentary committee – bound by Chatham House rules of confidence. Again, there was no constitutional obligation to do so.

Conversely, Syriza held a very high-profile public meeting outlining total opposition to the fascists, where Philis was billed to speak, to mark the opening of the Golden Dawn trial. There was a Syriza presence on the 4,000-strong demonstration organised by the KEERFA anti-fascist coalition, the ADEDY public sector union federation, the Communist PAME trade union front and others outside the court. Further, the justice minister in May acceded to the call from the Jail Golden Dawn initiative and anti-fascist movement for the trial to take place in central Athens, rather than inside the prison of Korydallos. That would allow proper access for journalists and observers, and also make it easier for the anti-fascist movement to maintain a permanent presence outside what was set to be a process lasting over a year. So what was going on with the contradictory decisions of different ministers and leading figures?

It partly reflected the loss of strategic direction which characterised the government from March into early April as it became clear that there would be no quick deal arising from the process it had signed up to, and which threatened to drain its initiative, political reserves and cohesion. It was also within Syriza, as a governing force, an expression of a line held by much of the old political class. So the mayor of Athens, George Kaminis of the centre left, and the governor of the prefecture, Syriza's Rena Dourou, had each given Golden Dawn councillors offices and all the other facilities and privileges. Both sought to justify doing so with very dangerous arguments. They did not claim that they had no legal alternative (disputable). They argued it is the *correct thing* to treat the fascists thus, because the left should be seen to uphold the 'rule of law', that the fascists will be beaten through debate and that taking specific action against them will turn them into martyrs for free speech. These arguments had been rejected in the wake of Pavlos Fyssas's murder not only by the radical left but, under the pressure of the tens of thousands in the streets, even by centre-right newspapers.

Now, much of the establishment was retreating from that position of refusing to treat the fascists as a normal part of political life. That pressure was expressed inside the government. And it was the more pronounced the more that ministers saw themselves as just another government. There was a range of theoretically articulated strategies within Syriza. But, at least in theory, what was common to all was an emphasis on mass mobilisations and on the transformation of the old state structures and ways of doing things. That was what marked out the party as being different from just a traditional administration with some novel policies.

Until mid May and the return of some significant strikes and protests, there was some truth to the claim that there was little by way of workers and anti-austerity mobilisation on which to base that second limb of a two-fold strategy for the left. But that was far from the case in terms of the mobilisation of social forces on the anti-fascist and anti-racist front. The mess made of the vote on the humanitarian relief bill took place just days before militant anti-racist and anti-fascist demonstrations in Athens and other cities on 21 March. Thousands from the new immigrant communities took part. As we entered Syntagma Square, on a route well trodden over the years, there was a new sentiment behind the slogans demanding legalisation of immigrants, the closure of the detention camps, the jailing and smashing of Golden Dawn and the lifting of austerity. Looking across the square to the parliament there was a realisation that, unlike over the last seven years, there were friends of the movement among the ranks of the government party – among the 149 MPs of Syriza. The spirit on the march was one of encouraging of the government to act. It would be supportive of it when it did, but impatient at unnecessary delay and compromise with the *ancien regime*. The demonstration was not marked by hostility to the government. But nor were people in a mood of desperate supplication.

While no irrevocable choice at a fork in the road was made during that unseasonably wet and cold March, there became apparent in outline two divergent paths in the labyrinthine overgrowth. The alternative illuminated by that demonstration may well be historically the one less travelled by – but it was real. It was there for all to see and to weigh in the succession of choices over how to proceed. That is, of course, should they choose to look carefully at what was ahead of them. For most, that was through the lens of the all-encompassing conflict between the Greek government and the Troika. But that confrontation was itself consequential upon the fundamental clash within Greek society – between popular poor Greece, and a wealthy elite. That became apparent in July, when the government's efforts to square the circle of negotiating an end to austerity, or at least its amelioration, within the confines of the eurozone and EU, forced it down the path of summoning up the kind of popular movement upon which its election had depended in the first place. And that movement laid bare not only the divisions of wealth and standing in Greek society, but also of power – above all the power of the unelected state structures, which had served the business and wealthy classes so well.

CHAPTER SIX

Face to Face with the Deep State

One of the first concerns of the left in Greece and internationally when Syriza took office was what the response would be of the permanent, unelected bureaucracies of the state. The question of how a radical party of the left should deal with concentrations of power historically aligned in personnel and structure to the business class and capitalist order was posed at two levels.

First, there was the classic debate among socialists over whether it is possible for a radical left force to use the existing machinery of government in order to achieve socialist outcomes, which those structures were honed in opposing. That brought back to life a set of theoretical issues among Marxists which had last been centre-stage in the 1970s in the wake of the coup which overthrew the radical reforming government of Salvador Allende in Chile and as part of the evolution of the strategy of the dominant strand of the Communist parties in most of Europe. Eurocommunism encompassed a range of political and theoretical positions. But they all shared to a greater or lesser degree the view that socialism was to come through the democratic – that is parliamentary – road, and that, while there were certainly condensed within the state apparatus powerful pro-capitalist interests, the modern, liberal democratic state as a whole was not simply an instrument in the hands of the employing class and political right. Rather, it was a field of competing class interests. So the struggle of the working class and of the left basing itself upon it was to be conducted largely within the state machine, not against it, even if that battle required repeated buttressing with popular mobilisations at certain points from without. The most sophisticated Marxist theorist of the 1970s Eurocommunist strategy was the Greek sociologist

Nikos Poulantzas. [That Greece became in 2015 the first country in which a government broadly of the Eurocommunist tradition came to office under its own colours (as opposed to, for example, the participation as a junior coalition partner by the Communist Party of France in François Mitterrand's government between 1981 and 1984) further piqued interest in Poulantzas's ideas. In the weeks following the Syriza triumph, interest rose in his exchanges in the 1970s with Marxists – such as Henri Weber, who then was one – who articulated the position of the early Communist movement following the Russian Revolution. That was that the state – at least in its repressive core – was fundamentally not reformable and that there had to be a final reckoning with it, based upon an alternative power – one which would have to overthrow the old in an act of insurrection.]

Now, critical as I believe the historic debate remains – which has recurred within the socialist movement for over a century – it can often take on something of a timeless and overly abstract character when left at a level of theoretical generality. That it is not the terrain of this book. The principal reason for this is that, in coming to office, Syriza posed issues much more immediate and more widely understood than the 'State Debate', as Marxist theorists had referred to their strategic dispute of the 1970s. The advent of a government of the left raised the specific question, asked by fairly wide layers of the working-class, youth and social movements in Greece, of what to do about the actual Greek state and its particular, anti-democratic features. While it may be related to the grand strategic question of how to achieve socialism – and I would argue that, indeed, it is – this second level at which the question of the state was posed was around the eminent practicality of how to end austerity and introduce limited social and civil libertarian reforms. And that meant dealing with the extant Greek state and machinery of government, deciding concrete policies and determining who would occupy which ministerial positions to oversee their implementation.

The para- or deep state

Not just Marxists, but even the script-writers of the 1980s popular BBC comedy series *Yes, Minister* identified a source of continuity of state power and decision-making in the permanent, hierarchical bureaucracies of the senior civil service, army, police, judiciary, university heads, public broadcasting chiefs and so on – all connected by revolving door to sinecures in the corporate boardroom. In Greek popular consciousness, however, the term 'deep state' means something more than just those deeply ensconced mechanisms of government and state administration. It refers to particular networks, buried within the state and traversing its components, which do more than simply preserve that structure and its interests. Their political leanings are more tightly defined than just an inherent sympathy for those of the class from which they are largely drawn. They have a propensity to intervene directly in politics in a way which bursts the constitutional limits which are meant to bind them only to do so *in extremis*, against a military threat from without or an insurgent revolutionary one from within. It is not just that they act to preserve a broad, capitalist, status quo. The status quo they uphold is narrow and serves the interests of very particular elites, which are often the hubs of powerful families and their patronage networks.

Perhaps the most vivid illustration of what the deep state means in Greek popular consciousness is provided not from Greece but from Turkey. The two countries' antagonism across the Aegean over the decades has brought mutual denunciations and opposing petty-nationalist prejudices. Those obscure what are, in fact, very similar developments of their respective state structures, particularly of their repressive apparatuses.

In November 1996 a car crash took place in Turkey during a grisly peak in the internal war against the Kurdish national movement and under the short-lived Islamist government of Necmettin Erbakan. It was to be overthrown the following year after just 12 months in office through a 'soft coup' supported by the military. As firefighters snipped the victims from the wreckage they uncovered the twisted body of a deep state nexus, which, just like its Greek counterpart, had for decades frustrated and undermined any government which had impinged on its core interests and of those whom it served. In one mangled vehicle were the bodies of the deputy chief of the Istanbul police, a contract killer for the fascist Motherland Party (MHP), who was wanted by Interpol, and a Kurdish quisling warlord who had thrown his lot in with the state's war of assassination against the PKK national Kurdish party. State, fascism, organised crime and anti-leftist terrorist force – all in one highway pile-up near a town called Susurluk.

At the time of writing, there had yet to be so illustrative and accidental an expression of the Greek equivalent of that Turkish deep state nexus. Decade after decade of scandals, however, involving organised crime, the military-industrial complex, conspiracies by the security services, killing with impunity by specialist police battalions and the cordial relations between the mainstream and fascist right, paint a similar vivid picture. It is captured well in Costa-Gavras's classic film *Z*, based on the novel of the same name by Vassilis Vassilikos. Shooting in 1969 and in exile from the Colonels' dictatorship, Costa-Gavras tells the story of the 1963 assassination of Grigoris Lambrakis, a member of parliament for EDA, the United Democratic Left, which was the legal cover for the banned Communist Party. The movie opens with his murder at the hands of a pillion passenger on a motorised tricycle who clubs Lambrakis to the ground as he leaves an anti-war meeting in Thessaloniki. The heroic interception of the assailants by a passing motorist, Manolis Hatziapostolou, changes the course of history. The police, army officers and far right forces who were behind the attack had hoped the murderers would escape. The police on the scene certainly did little to stop them. The assassination could then be blamed on anonymous 'indignant' citizens, who were venting their outrage at the treacherous Communist left. 'Indignant citizens', was to become a favoured *nom de guerre* over succeeding decades for what was in fact not spontaneous 'popular' violence against the left, but carefully orchestrated terror by the radical right.[24] The film then centres on the judicial battle by conscientious liberal prosecutors and judges to bring the full conspiracy – the deep state – to light.

As with the weaknesses of the Greek economy revealed by the post-2008 crisis, the dogma of liberal modernisation held these deformations of Greek democracy to be rooted in either some authoritarian national characteristic or in a failure to embrace modern capitalism so historically rooted as to amount to much the same thing. It is true that the way in which the Greek state expanded from the start of the war of national independence in 1821 put a premium upon a strong central administration. Over the next century, further diverse territories were added and their localist identities and autonomous governance had to be battened on to a state machine centred upon Athens. But Greece was hardly unique – certainly in the Balkans – in its path to nation-state formation. The overweening role of the military, and latterly a highly militarised police force and supine judiciary in the direct exercise of political power has more recent origins – in the civil war of the 1940s and the right-wing regimes which dominated until the 1980s.

The civil war state

Throughout Western Europe the purging of wartime Nazi and fascist collaborators took second place to securing the continuity and rescue of state machines, which faced popular forces demanding a radical shift to the left and a rupture with the politics and politicians of the disastrous 1930s. The gap in Greece between the promise of a partisan movement, which had liberated the country, and the re-imposition of an old ruling elite, which had either fled the country or often collaborated with the occupation, was the most extreme of any European country allocated to the 'Western sphere of influence' in the agreements between the wartime Allied powers. The result was the civil war. As we have seen, it was anything but a purely Greek affair. The royalist camp had traipsed through the Middle East during the war as an appendage of the British Ninth Army. It enjoyed the full support of, first, their old ally the British establishment and, second, the now dominant world power, the US. Within Greece, the returning royal court and pre-war political elite depended militarily in the war against the Communists and the left upon outright collaborators with Nazi occupation. In Greece that occupation had been more brutal than anywhere outside of Poland and the Soviet Union.

One result of that was that a short-lived period of administrative purging of Nazi collaborators in 1944–5 gave way in the 1950s, following the right's victory in the civil war, to a large number of acquittals and an amnesty for the many yet to face trial. Where that process most left its mark was on the military. First, though a small country in its population, Greece astonishingly had the largest military apparatus in Western Europe in 1950. Second, its officer and non-commissioned cadre comprised large numbers of collaborators plus the highly organised and political 'Holy Unity of Greek Officers' – IDEA. That organisation within an organisation – a prototype of a para-state or deep state – had been forged to suppress Greek troops stationed in the Middle East in 1943 and 1944 when they mutinied, expressing Communist sympathies and a desire to join the national liberation movement in Greece rather than assist the British in holding on to their Arab imperial possessions – such as Palestine and the throne of Egypt. The 'Drifting Cities' trilogy by one of Greece's greatest novelists, Stratis Tsirkas, is set in Jerusalem, Cairo and Alexandria and beautifully describes how this nascent civil war was played out in the area of the Eastern Mediterranean that was home to an old Greek diaspora.

IDEA launched a failed coup in 1951 and was forced to disband in that form. But its various tentacles continued to exert an influence and to reproduce themselves throughout the military. The army – the professional core boosted by national service, which continues to this day – remained grossly disproportionate to the rest of the state in size and, as we shall see, in the share of national economic output it consumed. One outgrowth of IDEA was the so-called 'Pericles Plan', a violent coordination within the military and police, extending to the civil, political arena, to destroy any growth of left-wing influence in society. The plan was activated after the United Democratic Left did unexpectedly well in elections in 1958, despite the fact that the leadership of the Communist movement and tens of thousands of its members were in exile, either in the Soviet Union and Eastern Europe, or on specially designated Greek islands. The murder of Grigoris Lambrakis was one result; the coup of 21 April 1967, another.

As in the 1940s, the Junta's fall in 1974 brought only a limited purge of the military. One particular avenue of continuity was the Greek military police, which had been founded in 1951. Anti-Communist fervour was concentrated in its ranks. During the Junta it worked closely with the State Intelligence Service (KYP) and became an extensive paramilitary organisation responsible for much of the torture and extra-judicial execution of those years. Under the post-Junta government of Constantine Karamanlis, the vast majority of the old military apparatus stayed in place, with just the figureheads of a regime which had enjoyed deep wells of support within the state and the Greek business class put on trial. The networks of the deep state had thickened and hardened in the dictatorship years. They were not simply vestigial in the years of the *metapolitefsi*. The 1970s and 1980s were decades of acute class and political conflict. As we have seen, the newly formed parties of the centre right and centre left, New Democracy and Pasok, proved effective both as vehicles for the rival clans – Karamanlis and Papandreou – who had vied for leadership of the country since the 1940s and also as mechanisms for incorporating that schism at the top, and the class and social conflict below, into an apparently stable political settlement. The unbanning of the Communist Party had a dual impact. It allowed the public expression and organisation of left-wing politics, but it also accelerated those tendencies which had developed since the 1950s towards a socialist strategy based upon parliamentary elections rather than insurrection or the civil war methods, which Greek Communism had been forced to adopt at the end of the Second World War.

Nevertheless, the fall of the Junta unleashed a huge wave of militancy, ranging from struggles by newly organising trade unions, to youth and student movements. The Polytechnic Uprising of 1973 and student resistance to the dictatorship had ensured that the universities were one of the few areas of public life where the purge of pro-Junta elements was quite thorough. The radical and revolutionary left of various doctrines – Maoist, anarchist, guerrilla, less so Trotskyist – grew significantly. The old national conservative right felt its power slipping away. Karamanlis's New Democracy provided a political home. But they had to cohabit with modernising capitalist forces, which in the 1960s had been organised in an opposing liberal party. Karamanlis faced a failed coup attempt in February 1975 aimed at restoring the Junta. And as the decade wore on, Pasok remorselessly advanced on the centre right. That resulted in high levels of political violence unleashed against the radical left and related militant social movements, such as among school students. In such an atmosphere, the old connections between the deep state, big business and the far right, far from becoming residual found new constellations. And these were to ensure their further reproduction.

It is in this period, for example, that the later leader of Golden Dawn, Nikolaos Michaloliakos, was arrested, in 1978, while serving in the military for smuggling high explosives to a far right outfit. There was a proliferation of veterans associations, 'free' pupils and students movements, associations of the 'victims of Communist terror' and the like, which spanned the ranks of the repressive elements of the state, the base of New Democracy and the radical right. They could furnish some ideological continuity, with the ideas going as far back as the Metaxas dictatorship of the 1930s. An ongoing organising and quasi-political role, however, depended upon more than a community of ideas. It was provided by the Karamanlis government and continued by Papandreou, despite some modest reform.

One of Karamanlis the democrat's first decisions was to fashion an elite battalion of riot police out of the general Greek force. The composition of the MAT, as it became known, flowed from its purpose. Designed for shock deployment against street and social protests – which were overwhelmingly of the left – it attracted those with the ambition to crack the skulls of socialist demonstrators. That psychopathic feedback loop was shared with the reproduction over time of the French CRS, Italian Carabinieri, British Special Patrol Group and similar forces. The anti-democratic civilian politics of Greece in the post-war years provided an additional authoritarian twist.

Greek politics and society were unique in the 1950s and 1960s in that they were regulated by a 'dual constitution'. Formally, there existed a civil and penal code which guaranteed the rights of citizens enshrined in the UN and in post-war, European institutions. But in parallel was a constitutional exclusion of the left and abrogation of the rights of those held to be subversive of the state.[25] In addition to the legal ban on the Communist Party, left-wing sympathisers were systematically excluded from all sorts of public employment and their civil rights restricted on account of their (sometimes imputed) political beliefs. The state of actual civil war of the 1940s continued as what would later be known as a 'state of exception' throughout the post-war years, which were proclaimed by liberal proponents of Western capitalism as decades of rising prosperity and greater personal freedom. That resulted in an enormous right-wing preponderance among head teachers, lawyers, judges and – even more so – among the police.

Until the Papandreou governments of the 1980s there was barely even a rule-governed national mechanism for recruitment into the police. Instead, power over both recruitment and preferment rested with local chiefs. The decisions tended to hinge on right-wing ideology, patronage and, often, family connection to powerful local economic interests. The charge of 'clientelism' to describe such practices, however, really enters the political lexicon only later, when Pasok took some measures aimed at ensuring that senior officers were at least loyal to something called democracy. That, perforce, entailed recruiting some figures who were politically aligned with Pasok. There is little doubt, as the later sorry tale of corruption in state procurement and other areas was to reveal, that there was some element of 'jobs for the boys'. But clientelism has proven to be a politically loaded term. It was deployed increasingly in the Pasok years, while the right-wing monopoly on state employment which preceded them has at best been taken as a variant of the same phenomenon, a Greek national disease infecting right and left. At worst, it was held as an un-interrogated norm. By implication, the image conjured up by 'clientelism' became a grubby Pasok party machine. That was certainly so in the modernising liberal media and in branches of academia. Unconnoted by the term are the likes of 1960s patrician and shipping magnate Aristotle Onassis. He cultivated an image of patriotic philanthropy in an increasingly celebrity-obsessed media. Tellingly, Onassis made hundreds of millions of dollars under the dictatorship and based his charitable foundation in the tax haven of Liechtenstein. With a low corporate tax base, threadbare welfare state and proliferation of politically partial foundations, Greece in the early 1970s prefigured today's neoliberal nostrums rather than embodying some national cultural resistance to Thatcher-Blair free market ideology.

The deformations of the Greek, liberal capitalist state lie not in some Greek particularity falling short of an ideal, but in its very integration into Cold War, anti-leftist liberalism on the one hand and into modern, market capitalism on the other. The opening shots of what would become the Greek civil war were fired in December 1944, under the aegis of the British army, into a left-led, unarmed demonstration of tens of thousands. Some 28 people were killed, double the total the British paratroopers tallied on Bloody Sunday in Northern Ireland three decades later. The state of exception of the 1950s and 1960s brought the deep integration of the bloated Greek military into the Nato alliance it joined in 1952. The US embassy and its CIA station in Athens formed the third corner of a triangle – the deep state of the military and police and the royal palace comprising the other two – which directly intervened into the government and political process. Greece was one of the greatest recipients of US military aid. When the 1967 coup happened, with liberal Democrat Lyndon Baines Johnson in the White House, the support continued. The Athens CIA station chief Jack Maury was asked about the 'rape of democracy' that the coup meant in Greece. His answer: 'How can you rape a whore?' The Pericles Plan was little different from those signed off by Nato commanders, in various parts of Europe, to counter 'Communist subversion'.

Throughout it all Greek business boomed. It was unencumbered by the regulation and red-tape which were to be cited in myth as the reason for the severity of the Greek experience of the European and global crisis following 2008. The construction industry of the 1960s enjoyed some of the fastest growth rates in the world. The workforce – often recently arrived internal migrants from the islands and the countryside – suffered some of the highest rates of industrial fatalities. With effective trade unionism repressed, growth came through grinding levels of exploitation. One result of the vast inequality between the share of national output going to capital and that secured by labour was that high levels of economic growth were not enough to sustain working-class Greek families. Growth was accompanied by emigration. It was common for parents to decide which of the eldest sons would go abroad to send back as remittances a portion of a wage which was beyond contemplation in Greece. Four decades later, younger generations of the same families would rehearse those dinner table conversations.

The Greek state which was forged in the 1960s and 1970s remained largely intact into the 1990s and new millennium. That meant continuing high levels of political violence. In January 1991, the minister of education under New Democracy's Constantinos Mitsotakis, a moderniser, incited the police and the ever-shadowy 'indignant' citizens 'to reclaim the schools'. Two days later, the president of the governing party's youth organisation (ONNED) branch in Patras led a battalion squad to do just that. He murdered teacher trade unionist Nikos Temponeras.

A state of plunder

The activist base of the right maintained its hold on and presence in the repressive arms of the state under Pasok in the 1980s and into the new millennium. There was hostility to Pasok, let alone the Communist left, at the base of those state institutions and in that milieu. The decision-making senior state functionaries, however, recognised the domestication of Pasok as it became an alternate vehicle, with New Democracy, for continuity of the fundamentals. The career of Akis Tsochatzopoulos is illustrative of how the draining away of radical and class content from Pasok left its leadership as little more than another self-interested elite. Its apparently furious clashes with New Democracy came to resemble a modern staging of the old dynastic feuds between rival political clans or the schisms of the first third of the twentieth century between royalists and modernising liberal Venizelists: neither were committed to radical social change; both had their loyalists within the military-state bureaucracy.

From being the darling of the traditional left of Pasok, Tsochatzopoulos proceeded through high office to become minster of defence under Simitis. In charge of a vast procurement budget, he helped himself to kickbacks at the going rate. He was exceptional only in that he ended up in jail. The image of him in handcuffs became a leitmotif in the memorandum years of 'Greek corruption', as he was forced to appear to face yet further charges.

Few outside Greece looked beyond the photograph and headline. Had they done so, they would have discovered that the 'Greek corruption' was centred on a deal to buy submarines from Germany, the model of business propriety. Greece paid €1.8 billion, but for years did not receive a single sub. When they did arrive, these fruits of German efficiency turned out to have an irksome habit of listing so dangerously that the crew felt they were in a particularly claustrophobic and hair-raising episode of *Das Boot*, the classic serial about a Second World War U-boat which seemed always perilously close to ending up at the bottom of the North Atlantic.

The corruption was a European, Greco-German affair, as was that revealed in a major bribery scandal involving telecommunications giant Siemens' activities in Greece – one of many surrounding the 2004 Athens Olympics. And it extended beyond the interface between capitalist corporations and individual ministers. Desperate to meet the budget conditions for joining the euro, the Simitis government decided to take the cost of the submarine purchase off the national balance sheet and instead account for it only when the unusable subs were eventually delivered. Once in the euro, the successor Karamanlis government adopted the opposite accounting trick. By retrospectively allocating the costs to the Pasok years, New Democracy could claim that it had inherited worse national finances than assumed on first sight and try to shift responsibility for them. Such sleights of hand were later to be offered as evidence of Greek cheating in order to lie its way into the euro. But not only were these practices approved by the EC, the ECB and the European statistics agency, they were also applied to massage the French, Italian, German and other national accounts to meet the stringent thresholds of the Maastricht Treaty, which all of them had exceeded. To paraphrase the extremely well fed, erstwhile Pasok deputy leader Theodoros Pangalos, who claimed that 'Greeks had all eaten together' in the spiralling credit years of the early

2000s, Greece, other states of the EU and the eurozone institutions all lied together to launch the single currency.

New triptych – old order

Four decades of convergence between Pasok and New Democracy meant there was neither a need nor desire for the self-reproducing commanding heights of the Greek state to intervene directly in the political process. And they could do their business quite readily in the wider assemblages of their counterparts in Nato and the EU under either government. The hard right predilections within those institutions which stand guard over Greek state and capital domestically and internationally, however, remained deeply ingrained.

This was the situation Tsipras faced as he secured a coalition agreement with ANEL and signed off in the last few days of January 2015 on who would occupy ministerial positions, which are meant to be the political masters of those permanent institutions. Three ministries straddle the thicket of connections constituting the deep state: the foreign ministry, defence, and policing. Left-wing friends in the 1980s used to joke about Andreas Papandreou's appointments to those departments, saying that 'the only thing the minister will control will be the space within the four walls of his office'. Beyond that, left-wing ministers could expect nothing but frustration of their priorities, bureaucratic obfuscation or even downright sabotage by the Greek equivalents of *Yes Minister*'s Sir Humphrey Appleby. With his choice of heads for those ministries, however, Tsipras ensured that the left could not expect even to have control of the paperweight on the minister's desk. The theoretical and strategic issues of the classical socialist debate about how far you may go in attempting to deliver progressive change through the existing state machine were not posed in any direct sense. The reason? The ministers chosen were quite simply not of the left. In fact, they were faces of the deep state and its extensions into party politics. Far from being frustrated by bureaucracy, these ministers would themselves repeatedly frustrate the aims of the left within Syriza and its base. The later failure to confront the EU and other aggregate institutions of European big business was prefigured and flowed out of an earlier and more fundamental capitulation: to domestic Greek capitalist interests and to the state structures which had served them well for 40 years.

Kotzias – après nous, les Jihadis

Veteran diplomat Nikos Kotzias was appointed minister of foreign affairs. He had been a member of the Communist Party in the 1980s. That, plus the European media's *frisson* attending their still shocking realisation that a party of Communist provenance was in government in a European country, led immediately to sensationalist, Cold War headlines about Athens going over to Moscow. An *ostalgic* strand of the left, nostalgically investing some faith in Moscow as a counter-weight to Washington, despite the 1991 collapse of the Eastern bloc, acted like a concave mirror, reflecting back but inverting the mainstream image.

At a euro summit in Riga at the beginning of March, however, Kotzias refuted the notion that Greece's foreign policy could now be characterised as some kind of anti-imperialist rupture with the past.

'There will be millions of migrants and thousands of jihadists flocking in Europe if the Greek economy crumbles', he said. 'There is no stability in the western Balkans and then we have problems in Ukraine, Syria, Iraq and North Africa.' Awkwardly avoiding the word 'crescent' and its Islamic connotations (as in the alleged Shia crescent arcing from Beirut to Tehran) he concluded: 'There is a scythe formed.'[26]

In a 'war on terror' Europe, the intervention – carefully planned according to insiders on Kotzias's team – was guaranteed to press the buttons of both the continent's securocrats and its tabloid media. It also wrong-footed much of the foreign policy commentariat.

For them, the Russophilia of both Syriza and its junior coalition partner ANEL had been the analytical prism through which Greece's developing foreign policy tended to be projected.

Kotzias's speech did not fit that mould. It was congruent with a more realist and political reading of Greek foreign policy doctrine, particularly regarding the Middle East and Eastern Mediterranean: that is, a continuity of deep state policy, not a radical left challenge to it. Kotzias's political evolution says a lot about how those priorities are subtly maintained through methods which fall well short of outright coup.

He was a member of the Communist Party's youth wing and was responsible in the late 1980s for the party's ideological instruction. Though he was part of the split to the left when the party suffered its 'Berlin Wall' moment in the early 1990s, neither his nor the Syriza government's foreign policy could be read off from a simplistic Greek 'anti-Americanism', which successive US secretaries of state bemoaned since John Foster Dulles. As a diplomat and then international relations academic, Kotzias worked closely with Pasok foreign minister, latterly prime minister, George Papandreou at the turn of the millennium. He pragmatically adapted to the changed international architecture brought about by 'globalisation' and the deeper integration of Europe.

In addition to the foreign policy of Greece, his academic work specialised in the changed international relations wrought by the emergence of the Brics countries – particularly Brazil, Russia and India.

And it is there, rather than in the ideological tilting against Washington and Nato, which animated both the Greek Communist Party and Andreas Papandreou's Pasok (at least rhetorically) in the 1970s, that the Syriza orientation on a 'more multi-dimensional' foreign policy rests. Kotzias has outlined it in a number of works, including his major study of Greek foreign policy in the twenty-first century.

In arguing for rebalancing policy to put distinctively Greek interests more firmly centre-stage, while in no sense mooting a rupture with Nato, the EU and existing alliances, it bears a striking similarity to both the policy and academic work of another professor of international relations in high office in the region: Turkey's Ahmet Davutoglu. As AKP (Justice and Development Party) foreign minister under the prime ministership of Recep Tayyip Erdogan, Davutoglu provided the intellectual basis for Ankara's 'neo-Ottoman' turn. The doctrine was expounded in his weighty but popular work *Strategic Depth*.[27] Just as with Syriza's 'Russophilia', overly ideological and somewhat culturally determinist analyses of the neo-Islamist government of Turkey fretted over whether Erdogan, rebuffed from EU accession, would break from Nato and plot an anti-Washington course.

Davutoglu, however, neatly summed up the aim of drawing upon Turkey's 'soft power' in the region to enhance its standing in the Nato/European pecking order rather than break from it. 'The more the bow is drawn to the East,' he said, 'The further the arrow will fly to the West.' The greater Turkey's regional role – in the Levant, among Muslim Brotherhood oriented Islamists and into Turkic central Asia – the more enhanced its status within the system of Western alliances.

The new doctrine in Athens was a Greek mirror image of that. Though it was overshadowed by the immense economic crisis, which, in the summer of 2015, still threatened membership of the euro, Kotzias energetically propounded in the first 100 days of government where Greek policy was headed. The *après nous, les Jihadis* warning (which had a whiff of the late Colonel Gaddafi about it) didn't come out of the blue.

The Greek foreign ministry hit the ground running in February. Amid the whirligig of emergency euro-meetings it was extraordinarily active in articulating an ambitious policy over the Eastern Mediterranean. In fact, in an homage to Davutoglu, the strategy, endorsed by Tsipras, seemed to be to use Greece's military and diplomatic power in that region, resting upon membership of Nato, as part of the battle to stay in the euro and within 'Western' Europe.

So Kotzias proposed that European foreign ministers develop a task force and policy to protect 'Christian minorities' in the Middle East/North Africa region. With Greece as a leading force, he also invoked Cyprus and General Sisi's Egypt as key projected partners. In May, Tsipras and centre-right Cypriot president Nikos Anastasiades advanced the plan with a jolly three-way handshake with Sisi following a summit.

Kotzias and his junior ministers intervened throughout February over the abduction of Assyrian Christians in Syria, the murder of 21 Egyptian Copts in Libya and the threat to the monastery of St Catherine in the Sinai.[28] Syriza prides itself on its modern secularism. But the foreign minister has invoked the language of confessional division – pitching as defender of Middle Eastern Christians, as Turkey and Saudi Arabia pretend to champion the region's Sunni Muslims against Iran and the Shia.

The result was Islamophobic rhetoric. New Democracy's Samaras was more extreme in words and also prepared to win votes directly on the basis of anti-Muslim racism, to which he is ideologically committed. Kotzias's interventions, in contrast, were not the articulation of an animus towards Muslim migrants or a belief in the clash of civilisations. Indeed, Syriza – not least in its ministers with responsibility for justice and immigration – had a strong anti-xenophobic pole. In May, to their credit, Syriza MPs stuck to their guns and passed a law allowing the first legal mosque in Athens, despite coalition MPs in ANEL joining the fascists to vote against.

The Islamophobic rhetoric flowed instead from the *Realpolitik* of an extended region in which the Greek state – in Kotzias's view – sees an opportunity to draw on its own 'strategic depth' so as to enhance its position. That is why Kotzias repeated the 'Jihadi warning' several times, despite it alienating supporters of Syriza among the European radical left. It was also echoed by the defence minister, whose ministry

– by dint of Nato membership and antagonism towards Turkey – is closely bound up with the foreign ministry.

Similarly, in its relations with Russia, the Syriza-led government's policy was an extension of the settled direction of the Greek state, not some progressive rupture with it. In a sober, well-informed piece for the US-funded Carnegie Moscow centre, Alexander Baunov observed:

> All of Greece's post-1974 governments also proudly touted the special relations between Orthodox Christian peoples and maintained that Greece can rely on Russia's protection. Both the heir to the Greek left-centrist dynasty, George Papandreou, and the successor of the Greek right-wing leaders, Costas Karamanlis, never missed a chance to emphasise their special relations with Russia ...
>
> Whence this fear of Tsipras and his visit to Moscow? Why does he have to be Russia's Trojan horse in the EU? Why are the Europeans so unsure of their own strength? In fact, Tsipras is much more dependent on Merkel than he is on Putin. Why not make him the EU Trojan horse in Russia? Or just a mediator, as he himself proposes?[29]

Following several high-profile visits by Tsipras and his ministers to Moscow, culminating in meetings around the anniversary of VE Day on 9 May, that assessment seemed close to the mark. Some Syriza supporters had entertained exaggerated hopes that a cash-strapped Russia would provide friendly bailout terms for Greece as an alternative to the Troika's lethal embrace. They held that illusion despite the fact that Putin's government had done no such thing – and at what would have been far less cost – when actual Russian billions were at stake in the EU/Berlin-induced collapse of the Cypriot banking system in 2013.

'Orthodox Christian solidarity' from Russia amounted to no promises but instead to another long process of tough negotiations about potential Greek involvement in a Russian gas pipeline to bypass Ukraine and about hinted-at Russian purchase of Greek public assets earmarked for privatisation. Both had been under discussion – on and off – by predecessor New Democracy and Pasok governments. Neither conflicted with US policy nor, fundamentally, the EU's. In fact, the Greek government found a meeting of minds with the US administration as President Obama sought to draw conflicting regional powers – Israel, Turkey, Saudi Arabia and, in part, Iran – into a new concordat to deal with the threat posed by the Islamic State (IS) and by other forces emerging from deepening Middle Eastern fault lines.

It would be consoling to say that a lack of radicalism in foreign policy was but a small price to pay for the government conserving its energy to fight the central battles with its creditors and to deliver a progressive social policy. The problem with such solace is that the impeccably conventional foreign policy served to undermine progressive initiatives elsewhere. First, the Islamophobia projected through the geopolitics of Greece and Nato in the Middle East strengthened – through the rhetoric of the foreign and defence ministers amplified in the right-wing media – the forces of racist reaction domestically, which Syriza genuinely sought to confront. Nationalist tension with Turkey (see below) had the same result. Second, it boosted the confidence of the old order and its deep state structures that they could bend the new government to their will. They had ministerial allies around whom to construct a political wedge against more radical currents in Syriza. Third, and much more subtly than through tanks on the streets, the foreign ministry–defence ministry axis provided a contemporary paradigm, in the context of a government with the potential to lead to greater left radicalisation, for how the deep state could grow beyond the structure allotted it by the constitution and have a determined effect in blunting that potential and in providing ammunition for the forces of the nationalist right.

An excruciating example of business as usual came with a meeting of Nato foreign ministers in Turkey in May. In legend, Nero fiddled while Rome burned. The foreign minister of Athens joined hands with his Turkish counterpart Mevlüt Çavuşoğlu and the rest of their colleagues on stage at the end of the Nato gathering in a toe-curling rendition of 'We are the World'.[30]

Then in July Kotzias visited Israel. He told its bellicose leader, Binyamin Netanyahu, 'We have learned to love Israel.' This, from a minister of a government of the left, headed by a party which had had a strongly pro-Palestinian policy and culture. It was more than words. A week later Greece became the only country besides the US to sign a particularly close military protocol with Israel. It was negotiated by Greece's defence minister but agreed to by the cabinet as a whole.

The minister for chem-trails

Under the coalition deal with ANEL, the right-wing nationalist party's leader had to be sat somewhere around the cabinet table. Tsipras placed Panos Kammenos at the head of the giant ministry of defence. Almost his first act was to board a helicopter and head for the island of Imia (Kardak in Turkish) in the Aegean. Little more than a rock, disputed possession of it had in 1996 been a flashpoint which brought Greece and Turkey to the brink of war. Kammenos was not signalling imminent military conflict. He was, however, sending a message to his political base that, despite joining a government headed by the left, he was not going to allow his party's opposition to the austerity memorandums (on account of their truncating of national sovereignty) to dilute its national chauvinist platform. It also told the military chiefs that he would champion against internationalist-minded Syriza MPs their established doctrine of antagonism with Turkey. That had been and remains the main spurious justification for Greece spending an inordinate amount on its military. In mid 2015 it was one of only four Nato members to meet the high level of defence expenditure which the US had insisted upon in order to get other treaty members to 'pull their weight' and take some fiscal burden off the Pentagon.

Arms procurement has been an enormous drain on public finances and a state-corporate mechanism for the corruption of public policy. When Greece passed its first memorandum, it was the largest arms importer in Europe and the fifth biggest purchaser in the world. In the course of the election campaign Tsipras had thrown the generals a bone with a promise that he would not slash their budget. With Kammenos, the top brass were tossed a side of pork belly.

Kammenos began his political career in the New Democracy student youth in the early 1980s. The young Tories had a particularly macho and thuggish reputation back then. He was in one of the two gangs – the Rangers and the Centaurs – who dominated the youth organisation. They were not the same as fascist street fighters. But I witnessed at the Athens law school during one student union election in those years just how prepared they were to use violence against the left. In British terms, they were something of a physical force Monday Club.

He graduated into the ranks of the New Democracy parliamentary party. He remained on the hard right. He became particularly close to the ship-owners and was reported to be after the post of maritime minister in Tsipras's government – traditionally a more lucrative office even than defence. Kammenos split from New Democracy in March 2012 after it had flipped from its opportunistic opposition to the austerity memorandums and had joined the government of banker Lucas Papademos. Kammenos's political contortions led him down the road of kooky conspiracy theories (with added anti-semitism to boot). For example, he maintained that the vapour trails left by passenger jets were in fact 'chem-trails' of the kind produced by low-lying crop-spraying and that they diffused a soporific drug which had made the Greek people go along with a new German occupation of their country.

Accepting for an instant the questionable assertion that there was no alternative to coalition with ANEL, defence was just about the last post one would give him if, that is, you were set upon a strategic path of waging 'class struggle within the state' or a 'long march through the institutions'. It is not that Kammenos stood ready on a hair-trigger to play the role of Chile's General Pinochet and lead a coup against a left-wing government from the office of minister of defence. Greece was very far from that possibility in the spring of 2015. Rather, his appointment provided the greatest possible encouragement to hard right elements within the military and elsewhere, who had been rocked on their heels by the defeat of their champion Samaras. That became apparent on 25 March on the military parade in Syntagma Square to mark National Independence Day.

As they passed the parliament, the entire army special forces unit of OYK (roughly equivalent to Britain's SAS) chanted nationalist slogans about invading Turkey and hoisting the Greek flag above the city of Istanbul. Left-wing Syriza MP Vasiliki Katrivanou was one of those who loudly protested, saying:

> The slogans shouted by the Special Unit Forces during the parade are a direct provocation to democracy … It seems to me it's inconceivable … [they should] go unpunished. It reminds us how urgent it is to purge the military of fascist and extreme right pockets which remain strong. Impunity had fed them.[31]

A few years earlier a similar provocation by far right soldiers had indeed led to courts martial and punishment. Katrivanou raised the issue formally in parliament. The eventual reply from Kammenos was 'What do you expect our soldiers to do – carry flowers?' He compounded the provocation. But there was no rebuke from the prime minister's Maximos Mansion. There can be little doubt about the impact of that in the special forces barracks, among the officer corps or in the police stations.

The ministry of police and mob rule

Kammenos at defence might be argued as a necessary, if heavy, overhead to secure a parliamentary majority through coalition with ANEL's 13 MPs. The same could not said for the appointment of Yannis Panoussis as minister responsible for the police and 'citizen protection'. He was not an MP and would have no vote on critical parliamentary divisions. Nor was he loyally of Syriza. He had instead been allied with the pro-memorandum breakaway to the party's right, Dimar, which had joined Samaras's government after dividing the Syriza vote in the 2012 elections. His appointment was seen as reward for his role as go-between in the dying days of that government, when Dimar joined Syriza in blocking the parliamentary election of a new president of the republic, thus triggering a general election.

The first of a series of provocative incidents emanating from the ministry of police took place within days of Panoussis's appointment. A senior police commander issued a national memo to the effect that local forces would now have no option but to allow 'illegal migrants' to come and go as they please because the new governing party's policy was to legalise anyone who set foot in Greece. It was a deliberate and two-fold misrepresentation. First, it presented programmatic party conference statements as if they were the government's practical, workable policies, which had yet to be drawn up. Second, it distorted those conference positions themselves. What followed with suspicious speed was a duet of interventions by Samaras and Panoussis. They gave every impression of being choreographed. Barely had the memo reached police stations when Samaras's office issued a well-written and detailed briefing from which the media learned of its contents. Predictable headlines claiming Syriza had 'opened the borders' followed. Cue Panoussis stage right. He made nothing of the *prima facie* coordination between an unelected senior police officer and the right-wing opposition, which had just lost the election. Instead, he fulsomely 'defended' the government in such a way that he articulated a harsh anti-immigrant approach entirely at odds with the liberal positions Syriza's conference had adopted. In one go the incident served to (1) give a foretaste of the reaction the state and right were prepared to unleash, (2) boost the position of Samaras who was facing a possible internal leadership challenge, (3) allow Panoussis to voice a hard right position while (4) usurping the policy area which belonged to the committed anti-racist human rights lawyer and minister for immigration, Tasia Christodoulopoulou, whom the media sidelined in their coverage.

Panoussis followed that up with a press conference a couple of weeks later in the Peloponnese, the heartland of the national conservative right, saying that 'Greece could not bear more immigrants', again in opposition to the measured policy being developed by the minister of immigration, who was committed to closing the camps in which thousands of migrants had been concentrated under Samaras.

By the beginning of April, he had in his sights not just immigration, but the political compass of the government as a whole. He wrote an opinion piece in *Ta Nea*, a bedrock institution of the old, moderate centre left. In it he accused fellow ministers of creating a security vacuum on the country's streets. In a manner characteristic of generations of right-wing social democratic bruisers – such as Blair's Home Secretary David Blunkett – he puffed himself up as a man of the people against airy-fairy liberals who were undermining the police, army and good old-fashioned discipline. The immediate trigger was a theatrical anarchist incursion into the grounds of the parliament and an associated small university occupation. The proximate political target was the widely respected minister of justice, Nikos Paraskev-opoulos, who was trying to defuse a hunger strike by some anarchist prisoners and pilot through a law to alleviate overcrowding and appalling conditions in the prisons. This demarche earned Panoussis a mild rebuke from Syriza's chief whip and editor of the party's paper who said that he should 'remember that he is a minister and not a commentator'.

The following month, however, Panoussis plumbed new depths. He responded to news of the murder of a 4-year-old child and the arrest for it of her stepfather by saying that there was a 'code of honour' in the prisons and that the accused would 'probably soon be dead'. The manner and repetition of the incendiary intervention in the teeth of protest removed any shred of ambiguity. The minister of police and protection of the citizen was advocating, even inciting, lynch law, mob justice.

That he had demanded exemplary punishment of hooded youth in anarchist 'mobs' served only to illustrate how deeply right-wing his brand of populism was. It chimed perfectly with the mentality at the heart of a police force whose belief in a certain political order outweighed any commitment to 'the rule of law'. They had not had to mould him to be their champion inside the government. When he took office, friends of mine in the legal profession in Greece observed how, unusually for anyone who had never held government office or even shadow responsibility, he did not need to be introduced to the senior police and civil servants in his ministry. He was on first name terms with all of them. As a professor of criminology he had spent much of his time teaching police officers of various ranks. He was one of them and had even blamed, in part, the notoriously right-wing Greek media for public perception of the police as corrupt, brutal and right-wing.[32] According to sources in the civil service bureaucracy of the ministry of police Panoussis displayed in his first six months in office a keen interest in the operational decisions of the force, and not only broad policy – as is the usual remit of a minister. He took personal charge of the operation to deploy police to break up a small university occupation. Since the Polytechnic Uprising of 1973 it has been something of a 'red line' for the left that the police should not enter campuses. His micro-management of policing operations underscored the extent of the breach between the government and the radical social movements when, on the night of 15 July, as the parliament was voting through the first of the new austerity measures required to secure a third memorandum, the MAT riot police responded to minor provocation by flooding Syntagma Square with tear gas and forcing thousands of demonstrators – and hundreds of tourists – to evacuate to adjacent side streets.

What price for whose priorities?

At the start of April the weekly *Proto Thema* revealed that the Greek government signed its first military procurement deal, and the largest for a decade. It had agreed to pay nearly €500 million to US contractor Lockheed Martin for the modernisation of five planes for the Greek navy. With no discussion in parliament, as would be the norm, it had signed the deal and made the first €45 million down payment. While this was spread over seven years, there was widespread disbelief that €500 million could be so committed when Syriza's humanitarian relief measures had been whittled down to about half that, just a tenth of what had been promised in the Thessaloniki Programme upon which it had fought the election and which had been described by many on the left of the party as a 'red line'. The *Financial Times* reported how:

> Syriza's partnership with Mr Kammenos and his nationalist party is considered vital to maintaining the loyalty of the armed forces to a government led by former Communists – many of whom were jailed in their youth for resistance to the 1967–74 military regime. The military has lost influence as tensions with Turkey have receded but it remains a formidable institution in a country with a nationalist tradition.
>
> Greek naval officers, in particular, are known to be frustrated over budget cuts that have delayed overhauls of ageing ships, reducing the fleet's seagoing capacity.
>
> 'We've seen chronic shortages of spare parts and vessels being cannibalised to keep others afloat,' said one recently retired officer.[33]

This loyalty seemed an expensive one-way street as the government struggled to pay wages and pensions but found half a billion for the navy. There was a further twist, serving to underline that for the deep state it was business as usual and that it had forged coordinated relations stretching into a government it had feared as radical interlopers. For the signatories to the deal were not only foreign minister Kotzias and defence minister Kammenos – quite routine for a foreign arms deal – but, incongruously, Panoussis also. There could be no logic of constitutional administration for the involvement of the minister of police, but in that anomaly lies buried the precise point.

At about the same time, the New Democracy era governor of the Bank of Greece made a fifth flagrant intervention into the realm constitutionally reserved for elected political figures. His office leaked a document on dwindling Greek foreign exchange reserves and banking deposits on the eve of a fraught meeting between Varoufakis and fellow eurozone finance ministers. Some backbench Syriza MPs complained. There was an instant rebuke from the editor of the house journal of Greek big business, *Kathimerini*, which lambasted all criticism of 'respected Greek institutions', such as the central bank and its management. The op-ed column was sampled across the European media.[34] That is the same media which contradictorily maintains that the Greek institutions of state are 'overly politicised', 'clientelist' and 'corrupt'.

The permanent drama of the Greek government's confrontation with the institutions of the EU and eurozone concealed a more fundamental and equally conflictual subplot: its steady capitulation to the concentrations of power domestically and to the specifically Greek big business and elite interests it served. The European media coverage emanating from Brussels ignored this antagonism in Athens. That reinforced the strand of thinking on the left which also saw the battle over Greece's eurozone membership as, essentially, an inter-state conflict. But that battle was a displacement of the social and political antagonisms within Greece. The Syriza-ANEL government's pro-EU timidity in the face of demands, fronted by Germany's Angela Merkel, for yet more austerity would become apparent in mid July. The greater and more profound problem with its contradictory strategy was not its 'Europeanism', but rather its timidity, its social democratic and gradualist politics. And that appeasement of elite and state power, that reformism (to use a term from the perennial socialist debate), was evident before the capitulation of 12 July to the Troika. It was apparent in the earlier surrender to the interests of Greek national capitalism – at home, before, and as a consequence of which, it took place on the European stage, where Greek big business is a junior player in the chorus of the continent's elites.

CHAPTER SEVEN

The Maw of the Minotaur

The clash of forces between the opposing camps represented by the Troika and Syriza had, by April, led to an unstable equilibrium. One effect was to open a little space for the government to recover some poise and to press on with some promised reforms after nearly eight weeks of parliamentary paralysis. These liberalising measures – such as on prisons policy and citizenship rights for the children of some immigrants – seemed peripheral to the central question of breaking with austerity and reversing the collapse in living standards. They were, however, a part of the manifold political battle upon which depended any hope of realising the promise of the January election victory. The terrain of that battlefield was defined by four features.

First, as had become apparent in the week following its signing, the 20 February deal had locked the government into the payday loan trap described in chapter 5. That meant that in the grinding, interminable negotiations, in which the well-staffed and highly paid bureaucracies of the Troika institutions were past masters, the austerity enforcers held in their hands both the €7.2 billion outstanding to Greece under the terms of the previous bailout and the power to crash the Greek banking system at any moment. After the Easter holidays, and approaching three months in office, one consequence of that began to dawn on the leading core of the Greek government. They were not negotiating the detail of the now superseded February deal. They were now mired in a more extensive process in which the demands of the Troika were prospective – looking over the next year or three to force capitulation to a programme of privatisation, regressive taxation, slashing of pension entitlements and evisceration of employment protection as part of a third memorandum, whatever it might euphemistically be called. In addition to the disastrous state of the inherited public finances, compounded by an economy tipping back into recession, debt repayments due in the early summer and a predicted budget crisis for the coming year comprised a looming crisis. The retreat in February had done worse than extend the grip of the previous memorandum. It had propelled Athens towards a third one, negotiated from a position of self-imposed weakness.

Second, and in opposition, however, was a powerful counterforce to abject surrender. Here it made a difference that, whatever the limitations of its 'good euro strategy', and despite sticking to it in the face of its evident defeat, there was no intention or desire within the government to capitulate. While many a road to defeat for the left has been paved with good intentions, there was more than moral worth in the very widespread commitment at all levels of the party and government to Syriza's values. Intellectually they meant opposition both to austerity and to the wholesale surrender to corporate interests characteristic of the parties of European social democracy. The strategic path of socialist reform might turn out to be blocked but Syriza at least wanted major reforms. Social democratic parties across Europe did not.

A contrast with the British Labour government in the crisis year of 1976 is illustrative. It is not just that then Chancellor of the Exchequer Denis Healey took a loan from the IMF and began – to invert his own rhetoric of two years earlier – a fundamental and irreversible shift in the balance of power and wealth in favour of corporate capitalism. It is that Labour's initial defence, that it was done under duress, gave way rapidly to embracing the policies later termed Thatcherite or neoliberal. The tactical capitulations became a strategic surrender and abandonment of even the idea of a socialist alternative to capitalism. Prime Minister James Callaghan spelt out the extent of the strategic liquidation, 'We used to think that you could spend your way out of a recession and increase employment by cutting taxes and boosting government spending. I tell you in all candour that that option no longer exists ...'[35] Forty years later, Syriza was committed to the kinds of alternative policies which the British Labour Party, followed by its European equivalents, had abandoned. That commitment rested upon more than an intellectual critique of the evident failure of free market policies, laid bare by the Great Recession.

The third salient of the battlefield in early summer was the determined will of working people in Greece and of the movements of social resistance they had thrown up to austerity. The political expressions of that were the victory of Syriza and the enervation of the old parties at the general election. The shift to the left and the fraying of old political allegiances did not stop on 25 January. Politics, and the relationship between political parties and their social bases, is more complex than simply the aggregation of public opinion polling on a range of issues and then some correspondence between those and a party's policies. A range of often conflicting opinions are usually bound together in the votes masses of people give to a party, especially at times of acute crisis when they are looking for a way out of it. It is only in the context of the rupture between millions of working-class Greeks and the pro-austerity parties which had held their allegiance for nearly two generations that it is possible to make sense of the polls and other markers of mass opinion in Syriza's first six months. The Troika, Pasok, New Democracy and the Greek business class (which largely commissioned the polls and their often slanted questions and methodology) never tired of pointing to the majorities, ranging from two-thirds to three-quarters, for 'staying in the euro'. There were similar majorities in favour of reaching some kind of deal with the Troika. Yet, at the same time, there remained throughout this period large majorities for ending austerity and for the government's negotiating strategy, denounced by the corporate media as confrontational and risking exit from the single currency. Persistent, pro-euro majority opinion did not translate at all into support for the fanatically pro-euro parties – the old centre left and centre right or the vacuous, Marie Antoinettes of To Potami.[36] After six months in office Syriza's opinion poll support remained higher, and the austerity parties' lower, than at the January election. That was not the result of some equation by voters weighing their pro-euro and anti-austerity views and then finding in Syriza some reflection of a point of balance they had struck between the irreconcilable two. The political support was a condensed amalgam of varied mass sentiments into a considered trust and hope that the new government might somehow end the nightmare of the crisis years. So public support would spike when the government hardened its stance with the lenders, even though the logical consequence of a hardened stance led towards at least the threat of default and exit, which the same public said they opposed. Apparently stable measures of public opinion belied its fluid and manifold reality. In November 2014 the same surveys had found precious little hope among the Greek public. But following the political crisis in December, Syriza won an election with hope as its central slogan and by swinging towards a more combative, left-wing posture under the cosh of a red-baiting assault by Samaras. A public seemingly wed to a conventionally moderate, give-and-take solution had at the same time evacuated the political centre.

The volatility continued into 2015. It provided scope for those who sought to renew a radical left path, based upon popular mobilisations to break the impasse. Those seeking the defeat of Syriza as a radical force also smelled opportunities. The problem facing the restoration-ist forces within and without Greece, however, was that there was no alternative government to Syriza readily to hand.

That fourth, defining political feature highlighted a difference between Greece under Syriza and under Pasok, during its short reforming period of the early 1980s. In pressing down on the Papandreou government in Greece and on Mitterrand's in France, which was contemporaneous, the EU and corporate capitalism could rally behind an alternative governmental force in the shape of the centre right. Though defeated, the centre right in both countries back then was far from the crisis point New Democracy had reached in 2015. The balance of political forces, in parliament and in society, in early summer ruled out an administrative coup such as in 2011, when the enfeebled memorandum government of Pasok gave way to a grand coalition. The government enjoyed legitimacy. There was popular opposition to new elections, and in any case the pro-memorandum forces trailed badly in the polls.

[Reimposing austerity and copper-fastening neoliberalism, therefore, would require more than a war of attrition by the Troika against the Greek government. It would have to mean undermining the Syriza government on other fronts too. One way or another, Syriza as an anti-austerity force would have to be destroyed and a replacement to the current coalition constructed – one with a parliamentary majority and some social base. A coherent approach to achieving that emerged in April. It sat at the intersection of two ostensibly opposed ideological axes – social democratic, liberal Europeanism, and authoritarian, national conservatism.]

Anti-democratic twins

Far from being the guarantor of democracy and of civil liberties, the EU and Troika institutions, through the imposition of austerity on behalf of all of the continent's elites, systematically generated authoritarian and chauvinist tendencies. The reality of the crisis years was the opposite of the authenticating claim of the EU in the high period of expansion: the 1980s into the 2000s. There were in that period diminishing differences between the centre right and centre left over the extent of social democratic welfarism within the increasingly free trade area.

Where there was *ab initio* unanimity was over confidence that EU institutions would vouchsafe democracy, the rule of law and the liberal capitalist state in the benighted Balkans, backward East and other unfortunate recesses of the civilised continent. Even the 'oriental despotism' of Turkey was to become modernised through the beneficence of *echt Europa, l'Europe authentique*, proper Europe: a 'white' Europe, where 'whiteness by permission' was granted to those conforming to neoliberal orthodoxy; equally light-skinned Europeans of the periphery, however, were considered 'black' the more their national economies sank into the red.

It was possible for the political class in Greece in that period to point across the Aegean Sea to their slightly more eastern, 'blacker' neighbour to encourage an ideological compensation for the material burdens borne by the mass of Greeks. In popular circulation was a kind of 'psychological wage', to borrow a metaphor coined by black US radical W.E.B. Dubois: whatever the long hours and low pay, at least you were free, unlike the poor Turk. Since the onset of the Great Recession, the material burden has become unbearable. The psychological wage has also gone.

Democratic niceties were set aside with the imposition of the banker Papademos government in 2011. The successor Samaras coalition took to flouting parliamentary procedures and governing by executive edict rather than by legislative vote. The guardians of democracy and the rule of law in the EC and European Court of Justice did not bat an eyelid.

In response to the election of Syriza, Jean-Claude Juncker, the president of the EC, selected the year before with the procedural backing of Alexis Tsipras against Angela Merkel, said that the treaties Greece had signed up to were immune from such trifles as the Greek people's democratic will.

In April, an unnamed EU official spelt out the consequence. He told the *Financial Times*, 'Tsipras has to decide whether he wants to be prime minister or the leader of Syriza.' Marlon Brando in *The Godfather* could be no blunter. Another (unelected) official said, 'This government cannot survive.'[37] Whichever language the official spoke in, the English 'cannot survive' has a sinister ambiguity: will not be able to/must not be allowed to. In either case, the European bureaucracies were not empty fields for the interplay of 'transfigured class forces' or any other baroque theoretical fantasy. They proved monolithic in the war to grind down and to domesticate Syriza, to turn it into a harmless variant of social democracy, as personified in French president François Hollande and his prime minister Manuel Vals.

The scintilla of political difference Hollande, then under some pressure from Jean-Luc Mélenchon to his left, opened up between himself and the centre right when he was elected in 2012 rapidly went out.

Facing a resurgent right – and the ambitions of Marine Le Pen's chameleon-fascist Front National – he launched his re-election bid in the spring of 2015 with a wholesale capitulation to neoliberalism, red in tooth and claw. Gone were the promises of taxing the 1 per cent and cutting the working week for the other 99; in came pledges for full-scale labour market and pension 'reform', just as was demanded of Greece.

Amid the flux of European politics as the Syriza government headed towards a crunch point in the summer, there was no sign whatsoever of the centre left breaking with the austerity straitjacket. Among the most belligerent antagonists ranged against Athens, and against the working people of Europe, was Jeroen Dijsselbloem, the social democratic Dutch finance minister. Just as in the 1970s and into the 1980s, north European social democracy offered its services to the defeat of radical movements challenging capitalism in the south. The strategic problem they faced in Greece in 2015 was that the once great party they had supported to do that then, Pasok, had become a zombie. In May, it was polling barely 5 per cent and was €150 million in debt. Party managers had taken out bank loans in 2011 in anticipation of achieving their habitual 30-plus per cent share of the vote and therefore a commensurate share of state funding for political parties and access to the European Parliament gravy train. You might think that those who had demonstrated such staggering financial ineptitude would be a little shyer in offering themselves as the white knights ready to solve the nation's fiscal crisis.

Sp. earlier?

The fate of Pasok gave rise to the term 'Pasokification' (the first mention I recall was in Greek) to describe the kind of collapse it and the Labour Party in Scotland suffered in the British general election of May 2015. European social democracy's response to Syriza's success made it seem as if its leaders had positively embraced that process of annihilation of their social base. For it was from sister parties of Pasok that the loudest and initial calls came for Tsipras to move towards a national government with the pro-memorandum forces of the centre left. Not only in policy, but also at the ballot box, Labour-type parties in Europe had failed utterly those who had loyally supported them for decades. Now, when a party of the left committed to radical form had at last managed to win an election and lead a government, Hollande, Matteo Renzi & Co. set out to break it. They formed an iron front with Angela Merkel and the parties of the right at the European level, albeit with a division of labour, and conspired within Greece to encourage a social democratic break from Syriza to re-establish the decrepit pole of the centre left. Old revolutionary friends in Greece had often reminded me, over the years, not to underestimate the capacity of parties such as Labour and Pasok to rejuvenate themselves by drawing parasitically upon fresh waves of radical movements. Not parasitism, but murder and feasting on the cadaver has become the novel twist on that tired survival strategy. Zombie indeed.

Starting first in opinion pieces then moving to features and 'news', a concerted line emerged on the pages of the European centre-left press that the telegenic Tsipras should confront his left wing and, if necessary, split the party and form a national unity government with pro-memorandum forces. In the incestuous world of the 24-hour media, the comment pieces became the subject of reports upon which pundits could speculate and the overall impression could be given that what was in fact a hostile intervention was instead a journalistic reflection of reality. Joschka Fischer, the former leader of the German Greens, proffered his advice about the need for 'realism' and a clash with ideological fundamentalists. Fischer's realist leadership of the

Greens had seen him, as German foreign minister, leading the MPs of the party which grew out of the German peace movement to vote for the first deployment of combat forces outside of Germany since the Second World War: Germany joined the bombing war against Serbia in 1999.

There was no positive case by way of results for such 'realism'. So instead, the focus was turned negatively on Syriza's left wing. Panagiotis Lafazanis, the leader of the party's Left Platform and minister for energy, found himself, alongside others, the subject of jaundiced profiles. Much was made in the media about a story in mid March that the prime minister's office had singled out 15 'disloyal' elements in the parliamentary fraction. Loyalty to the platform the party was elected on and to its social base was much wider than those 15, however. Commentators who lazily invoked the Ramsey MacDonald option – after the British Labour prime minister who split from his party to form a national government in 1931 following the Wall Street crash – ignored some Greek realities in projecting barely remembered British social democratic perfidy. MacDonald had narrowly secured majority cabinet support for what we today call austerity. He split in order to form a more stable government. He took with him only a small minority of Labour MPs. The national government's strength depended on the considerable support the big business Liberal and Tory parties enjoyed. No plundering of history for analogies could evade the necessity of having to seriously destabilise and demoralise Syriza and its 149 MPs if a pro-memorandum coalition government were to be formed.

Hence the other axis, from within: anti-liberal and right-wing populist reaction. New Democracy leader Antonis Samaras had looked worse than his usual sepulchral self in the wake of the election defeat. He fronted out talk of a leadership challenge and by April had developed a line of attack on the government. He charged it with incompetence and weakness over law and order.

Two factors allowed some traction beyond the defeated right for the grossly hypocritical and false charge of incompetence. First, the chimerical character of the government – a coalition of the radical left and chauvinist right – led to tension. It manifested itself on occasion in contradictory statements by ministers, conflicting briefings and other media morsels. We have seen how police minister Panoussis was prepared to brief against the government. Second, the leading group in Syriza walked a tightrope between negotiating the demands of the Troika and the express will of its base and of the majority of the electorate to break with austerity. The enormous social resistance to austerity, state authoritarianism and racism had left its mark within the party. While there is a high concentration in the parliament and in the upper echelons of long-standing political figures – mainly hailing from Synaspismos – the workers and social movements brought fresh forces into the party. Despite the constitutional changes of 2013, when Syriza moved from being a federated coalition to a party with much greater levels of centralisation around the leadership, the political culture remained more plural than in the old social democratic parties. One way to create a more coherent message from the government was by returning to the course set and pledges made in its election campaign. What the establishment media and old parties demanded was the silencing of the left. Those who had voted Syriza had no love for the anti-democratic regimes of the old parties. But, with a mounting sense of national emergency, they did want decisive leadership from their government. The second line of attack by the right, and much more menacing, was over law and order, larded with racism and strong-state rhetoric.

There was a minor street confrontation following an anarchist demonstration, which ended up in Exarcheia Square, at the back of the Polytechnic at the end of March. I happened into it. By the standards of such things in Greece it was a piece of street theatre. A few burning rubbish bins, a couple of cars set alight, some ritualistic stone throwing from one side and casually aimed percussion grenades from the other. The following day New Democracy seized on it with an artful line complaining of the government failing to get a grip on 'hooded youths' who were running riot. The hooded reference was cute. A liberalising criminal justice bill was before parliament. One of its provisions was to abolish the brutalising C-type prisons, which the last government introduced as almost its final legislative act. The prisons and a hunger strike by some prisoners were the subjects of the anarchist demonstration. Some 28 Syriza MPs introduced an amendment to the bill calling for the scrapping of another piece of New Democracy era punitive legislation which provided additional sentencing for anyone who commits a crime while wearing a hoodie – the inspiration came from New Labour's hoodie clampdown in Britain. And it was among the thoroughly modern centre left that Samaras's otherwise discountable push was to find a resonance. Predictably, and with now customary alacrity, the ex-Dimar minister of police echoed New Democracy's spin. Pasok and To Potami soon showed that they were as ready as the EU bureaucracies to play fast and loose with the liberal principles they purportedly defend.

Prison reform in the nineteenth century was midwife to the birth of mass, liberal parties across the modern world. Social democracy in the twentieth century became the new home for those humanitarian principles. Moves by Syriza to end the barbaric conditions in the Greek prison system revealed the full extent of the retreat from those principles by the liberal and social democratic parties. The criminal justice bill aimed to relieve scandalous overcrowding in the prisons by allowing for convicts who had served a large part of their sentence and who were ill or severely disabled to complete their sentences under house arrest. One of those covered by the reform was Savvas Xiros, the former leader of the now defunct November 17 terror group, which had targeted Greek state officials and British or US Nato officers in Greece. He had been in prison for many years and was 98 per cent blind.

It was predictable that the right would try to make the general policy about that one individual. 'Left-wing terrorism' was a catch-all term for right-wing Greece to imagine a composite anti-Christ of civil war Communist partisans, street-fighting youth, actual terrorist groups such as November 17, the current government and even Pasok. It may still be the case today that, as a friend explained to me a few years ago, the activist, ageing base of New Democracy sincerely believes that Andreas Papandreou was the secret leader of November 17 while he served as Pasok prime minister of Greece.

Instead of distancing themselves from this right-wing authoritarian mythology, Pasok and To Potami embraced it. They opposed the prisons liberalisation. Worse, they did so repeating New Democracy's civil war era rhetoric about a government of the left 'going soft on terrorism'. In so doing, they put themselves in the slipstream of a much bigger fish than the minnows of the Greek parliament. President Barack Obama's ambassador to Athens, David D. Pearce, intervened, saying:

If Savvas Xiros – or anyone else with the blood of American diplomats and US Mission members on their hands – leaves prison, it will be seen as a profoundly unfriendly act … Greece is an important force for stability in the region, and has been a good partner for the United States on a number of issues, including law enforcement and counterterrorism. We believe this legislation is inconsistent with that partnership.[38]

By any measure of diplomacy, that was a profoundly unfriendly communique. And it completed a modern version of the triangle of reaction on which the business class and right wing had based their opposition to the left and the radicalisation of the 1960s. It now comprised: often social democratic European bureaucracies, the conservative right and its deep state articulations in Greece, and the US-organised Western security apparatus, revamped in the war on terror. That political axis required a social body if it was to dig into and disrupt Syriza and its mass support. Ongoing clashes over the operations of a Canadian mining company in northern Greece provided a glimpse of how that might be developed.

As we have seen, the open cast operations of the Eldorado corporation on the outstandingly beautiful Halkidiki peninsula had produced one of Greece's largest environmental movements. In March, some 10,000 people demonstrated in nearby Thessaloniki against the company, which was threatening to close its existing operations unless the new government granted it a favourable contract to extend open cast mining, which already threatened to despoil the whole area and put paid to plans for the local economy based on sustainable tourism. Unfortunately, the miners' leaders had turned the union over to serve the company. The police stood idly by in the run-up to Easter while miners, acting for the company not in pursuit of their interests as workers who would have to live in the same poisoned environment as everyone else, attacked protesters who had travelled to the remote area on the peninsula.

For Panoussis, it was not an example of US-style company unionism in collaboration with the local unelected state assaulting both people and democracy in the manner of the Pinkerton private security forces or a mafia-run wharf as depicted in *On the Waterfront*. He adduced the confrontation as evidence of a breakdown of law and order, just as conservative university managers were raising an outcry in Athens about the ongoing occupation of their admin building. The company and union together bussed the miners and their families to Athens to stage a sizeable demonstration. This particular 'workers protest' received generous and sympathetic coverage in the Greek corporate media. The minister with responsibility for the issue was the leader of the Left Platform, Lafazanis, a bogeyman of the right. What was in fact a deeply rooted social movement in and around Thessaloniki for green economic alternatives to corporate environmental destruction was presented as a clash between 'decent working people' and a 'dogmatic ideologue' of the far left. The miners' demonstration against the government was atypical. But it provided in microcosm an exemplar of how the anti-Syriza forces might find some social depth. For a left with long memories it also provided a sense of *déjà vu*. The anti-democratic right in Chile, burrowed deep within the military and state, had exploited the weaknesses and mistakes of the radical left in government in the early 1970s to build a populist base for its elitist anti-leftism, at one point mobilising copper miners in the cause of their bosses.

The frame of racism

Into this mix came news in April of a four-fold increase in the number of people 'illegally' entering Greece. Probably 50 per cent of them were refugees from Syria, whose first European sanctuary is Greece, and not illegal even by the draconian and racist standards of European asylum and immigration policy. In a breach of the *cordon sanitaire* imposed around Golden Dawn by the anti-fascist movement at the end of 2013, fascist representatives were invited by sections of the media to opine about the latest statistic.

It was Samaras, however, who led the xenophobic charge. He packaged the right's populist message into a political portmanteau. In one compartment was the ever scapegoated, often Muslim, migrant. Into the other could be stuffed all manner of claims about national chaos and humiliation, losing control of the borders, a breakdown of law and order. 'It feels like we are under siege,' he said. His image of law-abiding Greeks assailed by immigrants and by feral, anarchist youth was antithetical to the actual state of siege on the Greek working class and its government laid by capital, domestic and European. The right collaborated with those forces, but could not boast of doing so in the anti-memorandum atmosphere revealed at the election. So it sought to reframe the picture of social crisis in Greece within a thick mounting of finely carpentered racism.

There had been a working hypothesis among those Syriza MPs and activists for whom tackling popular and instituionalised racism was a central priority. It was that the impact of going into coalition with the Independent Greeks (ANEL) could be mitigated when it came to passing anti-racist measures in parliament by relying on the support of at least some of the centre left. Doing so, however, would run the risk of crystallising an alternative governmental bloc with the centre left, who would demand in return further moves towards a government of national unity and capitulation to the Troika.

Resisting that would mean strengthening both the anti-memo-randum and left-wing positions of Syriza and to press hard on both without making concessions. Forces such as the Independent Greeks would feel compelled not to oppose anti-memorandum measures – the alternative would be their likely electoral collapse, just as their predecessor LAOS had when it joined a pro-memorandum government. The parallel trap for the centre left was that its voters' attitudes were generally liberal and cosmopolitan. It risked rupture with its already diminished base if it did not support measures such as the bill granting limited citizenship rights to the children of immigrants, a slightly watered down version of the law passed under Papandreou but struck out by conservative judges under Samaras.

As explained in chapter 1, the idea of forming a minority government and pursuing a radical policy on all fronts had enjoyed slender support in January. The conventional argument that a coalition government with 162 MPs out of 300 must be stronger than one with 149 seemed unassailable. The actual path of that government in its first six months, however, revealed that it made progress only when its left was prepared to press its policies hard and exploit the multifarious divides among its opponents – chauvinist and cosmopolitan, racist and liberal, pro- and anti-memorandum. When it did not, it gave space for its enemies – who reached into the state machine itself – to coalesce, despite ideological differences. In the common effort to undermine Syriza, the centre left was prepared to play fast and loose with liberal principle; the right, opportunistically to pose as national defenders of Greece against the finance markets and lenders. Both were in fact committed to the Greek business class and to getting back to normal by constructing some new arrangement to govern in its interests willingly.

The strategic debate on the left about how to take power, and hold it and use it to transform society has a long history. In different forms, it undergirded schisms in the socialist movement in the tumultuous years following the Russian Revolution and First World War, in the 1930s over the strategy pursued by the Popular Front governments in France and Spain, and the course of the social democratic left and Communist parties in the 1970s into the 1980s. At the risk of simplistic over-generalisation, one pole of that debate rested on a posture of militant confrontation so as to win support through dividing and conquering opposing forces in a 'class war', with the term 'war' being decidedly operative. The other emphasised the forging of political blocs with others, who had a foot in both camps, in order to pursue a long-term strategy of attrition of the more extreme opponents. The first six months of the Syriza government did not totally settle that debate. But it certainly moved it on. For the radical left and movements against the old order in Europe it provided a living experience of it more vivid than the historical reference points. That experience created some pressures for convergence in practice among those sections of the left who shared a resolute commitment to breaking with austerity, even if in theory and tradition they cleaved to different poles of the historic strategic debate. Whether one was predisposed to pursuing sharp, revolutionary rupture with capitalism and its institutions on the one hand, or to trench warfare within them on the other, the practical reality was that the forces of the other side were escalating the conflict on all fronts in a combative and coordinated effort to break the left and destroy its governmental bridgehead in Athens. One consequence was that those who had based their strategy on the assumption that there would be time to pursue a course of incremental replacement of austerity at the European level through seeking allies within the institutions of the EU for an alternative based upon growth and redistribution of wealth were forced to revise that assessment. That meant renewed argument about Greece's relation to the euro and the currency's relation to austerity, to which we now turn.

CHAPTER EIGHT

Revolt, Retreat and Rupture

Claustrophobic. The walls on either side were closing in, narrowing an already difficult path. And in the half-light ahead some fateful fork in the road was looming into view. That was the atmosphere in Greece throughout the month of June. It overshadowed all conversations on the left. You felt it in everyday life too.

The second memorandum was due to expire on 30 June. That was also the deadline for a €1.6 billion repayment to the IMF, which, together with the rest of the Troika, was holding back €7.2 billion owed to Greece under the terms of the outgoing bailout. European news organisations sensed the denouement and sent senior correspondents to Athens. Alexis Tsipras told Syriza MPs that 'the real negotiations are starting now'. The months of summitry up to that point had, indeed, been but shadow boxing. There was no way for Athens to meet its IMF payment. The cupboard was bare. All that had been achieved in the period before 'the real negotiations' was further to denude Greece's public finances and, through making the earlier foreign loan repayments, to contract demand and shrink the economy. At midnight on Tuesday 30 June, Greece defaulted on its payment and went into arrears with the IMF.

The week before the IMF deadline, Tsipras sought a bridging arrangement and headed to Brussels to try to negotiate 'a comprehensive solution'. Despite offering a package of €8 billion of austerity over 18 months, he hit a brick wall. The Minotaur of austerity capitalism smelled blood. Angela Merkel was in no mood to compromise. Back in Athens, empty-handed, Tsipras made a televised address to the nation late that Friday night into Saturday morning.

He outlined how far he had been prepared to go to find a compromise (a bad one), but that he had been rebuffed. Then he dropped a bombshell. He said he would put the terms demanded by the Troika to a referendum of the Greek people – to take place just eight days hence. It was only the second referendum in Greek history. George Papandreou had flirted with holding one in November 2011. But he buckled to EU leaders, who have shown a visceral opposition to plebiscites, indeed to any democratic oversight, at each stage of the consolidation of the European business bloc, with Germany at its pinnacle, which is what the EU is.

Within 24 hours the government made a further announcement. The banks were to be shut and 'capital controls' introduced. It meant for popular Greece a daily limit on cash withdrawals from the ATM of €60.[39] Friends of mine were not unique among activists of the left that Sunday night in immediately phoning relatives who might be panicked by the news. They explained to them why it was the fault of the Troika and that they should not succumb to the fear it was aiming to instil. The bank closure and capital controls were forced upon the Greek government by the barely veiled threats from the ECB to crash the entire Greek financial system as a punitive response to the referendum announcement. The then Greek finance minister Yanis Varoufakis would later reveal that his contingency plan for much more robust counter-measures to the ECB's financial terrorism was rejected by Tsipras and his inner cabinet. Those reassuring calls to relatives and friends by left-wing activists were usually very short. The trust binding those social networks was far greater than that between the government and its electoral base, even though Tsipras remained popular.

For the government, calling the referendum was a negotiating ploy. According to sources close to the decision-making, the initial purpose was to secure a return to talks with the Troika. That was borne out on the Wednesday after the referendum was called, also the day Greece defaulted on its payment to the IMF. Tsipras submitted a further proposal, worse than the earlier one, and his office intimated that the vote would be abandoned should Merkel agree to re-open talks. There was great unease among the activists of the radical left, including of Syriza, at this vacillation. That Wednesday afternoon, Merkel clarified matters herself. There would be no talks of any kind until after the referendum result that coming Sunday. She was going for broke.

'That was that,' one Greek government insider told me:

It was on Wednesday night that Maximos [the prime minister's office] realised it had no alternative but to carry through with the referendum. Even then, the thinking was that it would be a narrow outcome. They were not staking their tactics on victory. Certainly not a big one.

The leading group around Tsipras swung into building a rally for the Friday night, resting upon those powers which come with holding governmental office. That was the official campaign. Beneath, something extraordinary was happening. Those three days running up to the referendum were characterised by a level of agitation, unity in action, common purpose and energy by the variegated forces of the radical left such as I had not seen in Greece since October 2011. That was when the revolt against the second memorandum broke the Pasok government.

It infected the whole of the left. That included the base of the KKE, whose leadership had adopted an isolationist position of abstaining in the vote. The rally in Syntagma Square two days before polling day transported older activists back to the 1980s. Tsipras said nothing remarkable. Reading it in transcription, it consisted of the bland language of national populism. But its intonation and style, and the staging of the event drew from a deep well of left-wing sentiment in popular Greece. It reminded me of being in the same square 30 years earlier, listening to Pasok founder Andreas Papandreou, before he became sullied and when he still had that *laiko* (popular), intelligent and witty touch.

At bare minimum 100,000 people attended the rally. The upper estimate was 300,000. The *claimed* figure for the alternative Yes rally was just 10,000. An activist friend went to observe the Yes camp. Though managed by the centre right and its business backers, it was fronted by the tired faces of the centre left – the former Pasok mayors of Athens and Salonika. That was testimony to the disconnect between New Democracy and the mass of Greeks. 'Outside their venue was a fleet of Mercedes Benz and BMWs,' my friend told me. 'No wonder they love Angela Merkel.'

As we headed home from the Oxi – No – rally on packed Metro trains the depth of the social defiance summoned by the referendum became clear. A group of boisterous but good-natured lads started chanting: 'Shut down the television stations [which were all pumping out Yes propaganda]. Fuck the eurozone!' And: 'No, no, no – again NO. To the euro and to Olympiacos!' They were young fans of AEK, a rival football team. Many supporters' clubs had come out for the Oxi campaign. This was beyond the politicised minority in Greece. The full extent of the social eruption was to be felt when the results came in on the Sunday night.

Although confident of victory, we were astounded as we watched the results. The Oxi vote won in every prefecture of Greece – 61.3 per cent across the country. In working-class areas it was higher. Perama, a poor and immigrant area of Athens, registered 72 per cent. By contrast, Filothei, equivalent to London's Mayfair, in the city's northern suburbs, was 82 per cent Yes. It was a class-based vote. It was also disproportionately female. That belied the right's 1950s-style propaganda predicated on the mistaken assumption that women were 'home-makers' and would be more fearful of the economic dangers inherent in confronting the camp of big business. And it was young. Fully two out of three Oxi voters were under the age of 30.

Walking down to the spontaneous victory rally in Syntagma Square, I stopped with a couple of friends on a street corner. They had seen a small patch of fascist graffiti. We waited for a few minutes while they dug out some unused stickers of the Oxi campaign to cover it over. As we headed back on our way, Marianthi said, 'We can't leave things like that, you know. Not now, especially. The left needs to be felt and to lead in every space. If we leave a gap ...' While jubilant, the activist left was already turning its attention to the period ahead.

In the square, and amid gleeful celebration, Panos Garganas, an old friend and editor of the socialist weekly *Workers Solidarity*, told me, as the news of Samaras's resignation that night as leader of New Democracy broke:

This is a huge victory. It is so thoroughly working class too. We received so many reports over the last week of small employers, some not so small, blackmailing their un-unionised workers with the sack if they did not turn up to the Yes rally and vote Yes. They bussed people to their rally. But here's one example: a group of workers in a call centre were put on the bus. They got to the Yes rally. Then they all marched down to the No rally. The woman who led that is 19 years old. She is the daughter of Albanian immigrants. She is also an activist of the anti-capitalist left. These are the politics we must develop at the heart of the Greek working class – anti-austerity, yes. But also anti-racist, militant and for women's liberation.

This is a great victory in round one. Round two is coming. Tomorrow. We enter it with a success. And the other side enters it without a credible political instrument under the direction of big business. This is the Greek political reality, however the government vacillates and whatever retreats it makes.

We joked together how we would miss Samaras – he was the best leader of the party of big business working-class Greece could ever wish for. Someone put on a sound system somewhere the great 'total voice' of Greek popular and left-wing music, Maria Dimitriadi. We sang: 'when the people rise up, *pios to stamataei; pios, pios to stamataei*?' ('who can stop them; who, who can stop them?')

Nassos, a member of the Prospert union at the re-opened state broadcaster ERT, said, 'I cannot wait to be in work tomorrow. Now we will see who runs the place.' A few days earlier, at a public meeting to build the Oxi campaign, he had level-headedly explained how the government's wobbling had demoralised Syriza supporters at work and had encouraged the old, pro-memorandum management, and those who had sided with it, provocatively to challenge the left. The referendum campaign was about more than a cross on a ballot paper. It crystallised the division of Greece into two great camps: hope against fear; working class against the elites; the downtrodden against their tormentors; a defiant No against a servile Yes.

Stathis, who works with young homeless people in Athens, made the kind of acute observation which finds its way into the official journalistic record only if there is a chronicler who listens carefully to voices at the base of society:

They threw everything into this. The whole of the media – Greek and European. Every old face from the old order. But it was a 61 per cent vote of defiance. That was with the banks closed and under financial siege. That shows the people will fight – when they believe there is a way forward and a leadership they can trust.

There are queues at the banks. But what the elites fail to understand is that for large swathes of Greece €60 or €50 a day is a dream, not an imposition. There are so many people who do not leave their homes, if they have one to call their own, because they have no money. Transport, a coffee, a bottle of water cost money. Because there is free transport, to compensate for the bank closure, these people entered the public realm again. They moved. They breathed.

The financial siege has an element of a state of war. And siege is a leveller, unless you are of the elite and beyond the rationing of scarce resources. So hundreds of thousands of people in this country have felt these days and tonight that they are not a separate underclass. They feel that they are in the same boat as those people who do have a job and a home, no matter what the debt and pressures. And so what Merkel and the elites have discovered is this: they can scream and issue orders as much as they like, but for large numbers of people, in Greece, and I think increasingly elsewhere, our ears are simply closed to their threats and blackmail.

As the referendum result sank in the following day I spoke to a senior trade unionist at the Piraeus port, slated for privatisation. A supporter of Meta, the Syriza trade union group, he said:

This victory is not only big. It is too big for the government. Too big for those who would deliver a capitulation.

There was an ambiguity in his words. Too big for their wishes; or so big that it would prevent them from an unnecessary surrender to the Troika? The ambiguity was clarified within the week.

Retreat

The first sign of the use to which the government was to put the Oxi vote came the morning after the result. Varoufakis, who had become a bogeyman for the other eurozone finance ministers, stood down, and was replaced by Euclid Tsakalotos. Varoufakis echoed the then united line of the cabinet: he was resigning so as to remove an obstacle to negotiations with the Troika: himself. An elderly neighbour in the area of Athens I stay in summed up the widespread popular reaction. 'He's a good man,' she said, 'He stood up for us and for the country. That's why *they* don't like him. I'm so sad he has resigned. He says it's for the best. Maybe that's true. I'm not sure. But I don't really understand politics.'

Despite endorsing the government's return to the theatre of cruelty which was negotiations with the Troika, Varoufakis let his true feelings be known, saying that he would 'wear the creditors' loathing with pride'. It was a sign of the rupture to come – not, in the first instance, between Greece and the eurozone, but within the government and inside Syriza the party, just six months into office.

The path to surrender was well lit. No one can take that away from Alexis Tsipras and the leading group huddled in the Maximos Mansion. He set out to Brussels with the Oxi victory in his pocket, and with a soon to be fulfilled tactical line. It was to accept the strictures of the Troika, but with the hope of militating against its excesses. On the Friday following the referendum the government tabled an enabling motion in parliament to delegate authority to Tsipras, deputy prime minister Yannis Dragasakis and the newly appointed finance minister, Tsakalotos, to head to Brussels and conclude a deal. There was a small, but important, revolt among Syriza MPs. Two voted against. Eight abstained (there is a procedure to register an 'active abstention' in the Greek parliament by voting '*paron*', 'present'). Seven did not attend the vote. Among those abstaining were the speaker of the parliament, Zoe Konstantopoulou, and Panagiotis Lafazanis, the leader of Syriza's left opposition and then a government minister. Varoufakis had voiced his opposition to the government's line in an internal meeting of Syriza MPs. Then he absented himself from the vote. The combined effect of the revolt was to deprive the Syriza-ANEL government of its majority.

Tsipras headed for Brussels, though, with a solid parliamentary vote behind him: the mainstream opposition parties had voted with the government. Within 36 hours, the outcome was a disaster. On the Monday morning, not eight days after the Oxi referendum result, Tsipras signed up to a deal which only the night before his aides had briefed was 'humiliating and unacceptable'. Like much of Greece, I had stayed up with friends until the early hours, listening to the news feeds as the full scale of what was afterwards described as a 'mental water-boarding' and 'crucifying' of Tsipras and of the Greek government delegation leaked out. You could almost hear the cries from neighbours: 'Walk out, Alexis! Tell them to shove it!' The Greek prime minister did not. He came back to Athens signed up to a commitment to the most breathtaking of concessions. They were but the precondition for the opening of negotiations upon a third memorandum. The details of the assault on living standards and pensions, of the surrendering of 'fiscal sovereignty' (that is the country's control over its finances), of the privatisation of public assets (which, thanks in large part to trade union and popular resistance, remained considerable) need not detain us. They will have been superseded by the time you read this. In any case, a leak from the IMF on the Tuesday after the deal was signed spoke to the central truth. The new austerity package would, the Fund's economists predicted, lead to the burden of public debt rising to twice Greece's national economic output within two years. This was no calculated, off-message intervention by the IMF. Its director, Christine Lagarde, remained in lock-step with Merkel and the rest. The IMF did have an alternative to the European model of austerity. But it was no less savage. Since the onset of the Great Recession, the Fund had favoured harsher measures up front with possible relief of debt obligations in the future. That the debt to be relieved was owed largely to the Frankfurt-based ECB and not to the Washington-based IMF was not lost upon German and French bankers. While it is true that the leaked document pointed to what would become more serious divisions between the world's leading economic powers, that difference of emphasis offered no crumb of comfort either to the Greek government or to the wider movement across Europe against austerity.

Tsipras broadcast to the nation, and to foreign leaders, via an hour-long televised interview the night before a crucial debate and vote in parliament to take place on Wednesday 15 July. It was the same

Alexis who had enthused us in Syntagma Square not 11 nights earlier. The balance – of content and of tone – however, had been inverted. It is too glib to impute some Damascene conversion undergone on his road to Brussels a few days earlier. With some aplomb he outlined his argument. This time directed primarily against critics on the left, rather than against the right and the Yes camp, upon whom he now relied in parliament.

The central charge he laid against the left, all but naming prominent figures, was that it had no alternative to the course he had reluctantly set upon. No one can gainsay how much I have fought, he said. But There Is No Alternative. That mantra of the Thatcher-Reagan dawn of neoliberal capitalism was, unfortunately, to be intoned by the Greek government and those who supported its actions over the coming weeks and months.

He spelt it out thus. Grexit (the obscuring, catch-all term for Greece leaving the euozone single currency bloc), he said, was a punitive measure, a threat brandished by German finance minister Wolfgang Schäuble. Tsipras confirmed those media stories since December of 2014 which had reported that enforced Grexit was, indeed, a cudgel which Schäuble had wielded on at least three occasions. Further, said Tsipras, Greece leaving the eurozone was the policy of Marine Le Pen and the fascists of the Front National in France. 'How can it then be a policy of the left?' he asked – and with some effect.

'That's smart. He'll win some ground with that,' said Soritis, a friend of mine of 25 years, as we discussed Tsipras's performance. He continued:

The whole way the issue is framed by the media and elites is a choice between either the austerity demanded by Schäuble, or expulsion from the eurozone, with a devaluation of a new currency and still with financial war against Greece. That is what Schäuble threatens as the alternative. We should reject that choice. If we accept those terms, then Tsipras's surrender to the devil you know can make sense to working-class Greece.

Tsipras's 36 hours in Brussels, followed by his success in pushing the deal through the Greek parliament, clarified, were it necessary, a half decade of debate on the international left about strategic alternatives to a Europe of austerity.

Euros, drachmas and Grexits

The Great Recession beginning in 2008 hit Europe particularly hard. A sharp banking crisis was followed by a slump and a feeble, low-growth recovery. So intractable was the depression that what had been unconventional criticisms of the euro and Europe's financial architecture now became more commonplace.[40]

The path chosen by the European and British elites to deal with the crisis was for each of the 28 EU states to take on the debts of the insolvent banks and then to impose austerity measures upon the public, using the totem of by now heavily indebted government balance sheets as justification. John Milios, until March 2015 Syriza's chief economic adviser, summed up the 'class logic' of continuing with the three decades of neoliberalism which had led to the crisis in the first place:

> The ruling European elites have thus voluntarily subjected themselves to a high degree of sovereign default risk in order to consolidate the neoliberal strategies. In other words, they have jointly decided to exploit the crisis as a means to further neoliberalise state governance. Member states are faced with the dilemma: austerity-cuts-privatisations or risk default. By and large, these are commensurate choices. Even in the latter scenario, member states would accept a rescue package, the content of which is again austerity-cuts-privatisations.[41]

That analysis was common ground among left opponents of austerity. This is not the place, nor is there the space, to review extensively the arguments put forward by a range of commentators reaching into mainstream economic thinking.[42] At the centre of those debates lay a set of questions over whether the euro was irredeemably flawed and whether, and how, an alternative to austerity could be pursued. Here I want to look briefly at that nexus of political and economic issues through considering the interventions of three prominent Syriza MPs and economic thinkers: Yanis Varoufakis; his successor as finance minister, Euclid Tsakalotos and Costas Lapavitsas, a trenchant left critic of the strategy pursued by the Tsipras government. Between them they represent three poles of the strategic debate about ending austerity in the eurozone and EU.

Varoufakis outlined his analysis of the way the structure of the eurozone created imbalances between a more competitive core, which exported more than it imported, and a weaker periphery in his book *The Global Minotaur*:

> The formation of the eurozone engendered deepening stagnation in the deficit countries plus France. It also enabled Germany and the surplus eurozone nations to achieve exceptional surpluses. These became the financial means by which German corporations institutionalised their activities in the United States, China and Eastern Europe.[43]

He went on in a paper he co-authored in 2013 to offer a 'modest proposal' to solve the eurozone crisis. Notwithstanding the structural flaws of the eurozone – principally that it created a monetary union (a single currency) but not an economic union (taxation and spending policy which may even out the imbalances between different countries), he argued that it was possible to exit the banking, debt, investment and social crises in Europe without fundamentally transforming the eurozone. He wrote:

The Modest Proposal introduces no new EU institutions and violates no existing treaty. Instead, we propose that existing institutions be used in ways that remain within the letter of European legislation but allow for new functions and policies.

These institutions are: The European Central Bank – ECB; The European Investment Bank – EIB; The European Investment Fund – EIF; and The European Stability Mechanism – ESM.[44]

The technical reforms proposed for those institutions need not concern us here. Varoufakis tried to explain them at length to successive gatherings of the eurogroup of finance ministers. He later revealed his exasperation that the last thing the eurozone finance ministers wanted to discuss was economics. Varoufakis was not a member of Syriza until the 25 January election campaign. He had been an adviser to George Papandreou. He became critical of the first memorandum and, in 2010, became close to Alexis Tsipras. His strategic approach – which may be termed rationalist reforming – was congruent with the modernising strand in Synaspismos. It became the line of the Syriza government. It rested on two assumptions. First, that success at the ballot box would be sufficient to force the Troika to take account of the Greek government's position in negotiations. Second, that the logical force of its arguments would win the day in the institutions of the Troika, such as the IMF, whose own economic forecasts demonstrated that austerity was not delivering the economic recovery which it purportedly was meant to.

The Varoufakis and Syriza-ANEL government position was modest indeed. Shortly after the election he stated publicly that 70 per cent of the second memorandum was not bad for Greece. Two months later he made explicit his view that what the government was proposing to the Troika was not a policy in opposition to business, but a pro-business alternative to austerity. He told the 20th Banking Forum of the Union of Greek Bankers, on 22 April 2015:

In the year 2015, after five years of catastrophic recession, where ultimately everybody is a victim, there are only a few cunning people who have profited from this crisis. The era in which a government of the left was by definition contrary to the milieu of entrepreneurship has passed. If we get to a point when there is growth, we can start talking again about conflicting labour and capital interests. Today we are together.

The Syriza government – with ANEL, led by Kammenos, who has been close to the shipping owners since he came into politics – signalled to big business at home that it would not impinge on its activities. Rather, it would negotiate at the European level for a policy which, it promised, was compatible with Greek capitalist interests. That strategic line of reforming the euro 'for its own good' ran directly into the sand.

A week after his enforced departure from the government Varoufakis gave a long interview to the *New Statesman*. He laid bare the complete refusal of the eurozone group to listen to argument and its contempt for democracy:

> [T]here was point blank refusal to engage in economic arguments. Point blank. You put forward an argument that you've really worked on, to make sure it's logically coherent, and you're just faced with blank stares. It is as if you haven't spoken. What you say is independent of what they say. You might as well have sung the Swedish national anthem – you'd have got the same reply.[45]

He also revealed how the Greek cabinet had voted down 'energetic' contingency plans he had drawn up to cope with the ECB's threats to crash the banking system. He was at pains to point out that they fell short of a 'Plan B' for full-scale Greek default on its debt and exit from the eurozone. Two weeks later, however, the Greek media was awash with what read like a witch-hunt of Varoufakis after the paper *Kathimerini* revealed a transcript of conversations he had had outlining a more robust emergency plan to seize foreign currency reserves and introduce a parallel currency in Greece to meet the Troika's financial terrorism.[46]

Speaking in parliament against the deal Tsipras had signed up to, Varoufakis invoked the criticisms made a century before by the British liberal economist John Maynard Keynes of the Versailles Treaty imposed upon a defeated Germany at the end of the First World War. Keynes had sat through Versailles negotiations in 1919 but walked out before the end and wrote a short book, *The Economic Consequences of the Peace*. In it he predicted that the combination of crushing war reparations and the incompatibility of the Treaty with the ostensibly free trade and economically liberal order which the victorious allies promulgated would lead to a second world war. That he estimated it would come in 20 years made his warnings all the more prophetic when that war did break out in 1939.

As his breach with the government grew deeper throughout July, there were good grounds for thinking that Varoufakis considered himself something of a modern-day Keynes figure. He certainly drew heavily on the British economist's theory. And his response to the aggressive moves by the Troika hinted at another similarity. Varoufakis could be seen as one of string of broadly mainstream figures – he was of the centre left, rather than its radical or anti-capitalist strands – who, faced with a confrontational crisis, had not hesitated to propose strong counter-measures, even if that meant sacrificing the interests of some capitalists – the banks, in this case – in order to protect those of the system in general. This was what Democrat US President Roosevelt had done in the 1930s. But in 2015, there was no Roosevelt figure either in North America, or in Europe.

Euclid Tsakalotos is part of a strand of thinking inside Syriza which went some way to explaining why. In his book *The Crucible of Resistance*[47] he located the inherent inequalities and bias towards recessionary policy in the eurozone as a more fundamental problem than just the malfunctioning of its financial institutions. The eurozone embodied in transfigured form the inequalities generated within its component states in the neoliberal era of capitalism. But, he argued, the failure at the hands of global financial institutions of earlier national attempts to bring progressive reform (he cited the British Labour government of the 1970s, and Andreas Papandreou's first Pasok government and François Mitterrand's first administration – both in the early 1980s) meant that any 'national break' from the euro would suffer the same fate. He summed up his book's argument thus:

> [We] argue that the left cannot ignore this experience, and in particular the inability of leftist national strategies to take on the might of financial markets … Any strategy of the left must incorporate supra-national solutions to supra-national problems. Only through the taming of financial markets can we create the space for democratic decision-making …

The eurozone could not be reformed through rational argument but was, like the domestic economy and society, a field of class struggle:

> [I]f Syriza is to negotiate a new deal within Europe it needs a massive wave of solidarity to begin to shift the balance of forces within Europe. For any alternative strategy needs to create space for its democratic programme of economic and social reform. Exiting the euro, and returning to a national strategy, would isolate us from those experiencing the same neoliberal policies elsewhere, lead to a return to the competitive devaluations of the 1930s, and cede the ideological ground to those nationalists who want to turn the struggle of working people in the whole of Europe for a new kind of politics into one of Greece versus Germany (or the South versus the North).[48]

Tsakalotos is part of a current within Syriza which stood between the Left Platform opposition and the leading group around Tsipras. It cohered around political positions put forward by 53 prominent figures in Syriza. They constituted the left of the 'presidential majority' backing the Tsipras's leadership. One admirable feature of the Tsakalotos position was its rejection of nationalism and its emphasis upon a European-wide struggle by the left and social movements against austerity and neoliberal capitalism. It was also strongly anti-racist.

But the experience of Syriza's first six months in office revealed two fatal weaknesses. The first was political. How was this 'massive wave of solidarity' to be delivered? There was, and always has been, great unevenness across Europe in the rhythm of social movements. In part, that reflects the structural unevenness of the EU and eurozone themselves. The fact that they comprise separate nation states also meant that the electoral timetables of each were not synchronised. In January 2015 there was much hope among Syriza supporters that the anti-establishment Podemos party would be able to open a second front in elections in the Spanish state. But the Spanish general election was not due until the very end of the year. The second weakness was in the analysis of the eurozone itself. The total inflexibility of eurozone leaders, even when faced with the possibility of a Greek default and exit, perhaps leading to a return of the financial chaos of 2008, pointed to the fact that its institutions were *less* susceptible to a 'changed balance of forces' than were those of the nation states which made it up. This was the substance of the argument made doggedly by Costas Lapavitsas, the Syriza economist and MP who had done more than any to advance a case for a break from the euro.

Lapavitsas and colleagues at the Research on Money and Finance group produced three major papers early on in the Great Recession arguing that it would prove impossible for Greece to escape the crisis while staying trapped within the euro. They were collected together and published in 2012 under the title *Crisis in the Eurozone*.[49] The third paper, 'Breaking Up? A Route Out of the Eurozone Crisis', published in November 2011 argued:

The euro is a form of international reserve currency created by a group of European states to secure advantages for European banks and large enterprises … The euro has attempted to compete against the dollar but without a correspondingly powerful state to back it up. Its fundamental weakness is that it relies on an alliance of disparate states representing economies of diverging competitiveness …

The result has been that Germany has emerged as the economic master of the eurozone … Austerity is contradictory because it leads to recession thus worsening the burden of debt and further imperilling banks and the monetary union itself. This contradiction is compounded by the nature of the [euro] … As a result, the [eurozone] currently faces a sharp dilemma: either to create state mechanisms that could enforce policies raising the competitiveness of the periphery, or to undergo a rupture.

In an extensive interview with *Jacobin* magazine in March 2015, Lapavitsas refuted the idea that merely changing the balance of political forces between the eurozone's governments would be sufficient to bring a break from austerity. The problem was fundamental and lies in the 'political economy', the very structure of the monetary union:

what is feasible and what is not ultimately is determined by the political economy of the monetary union … Now Syriza has just discovered that … If it wants to achieve other things politically, it must change the institutional framework. There is no other way. To change that framework, you've got to go for a rupture. You've got to go for a break. You cannot reform the euro system. It's impossible to reform the monetary union. That's what became very clear.[50]

He went on to summarise the policies he had long advocated for a 'Grexit' from the euro, the return to a national currency and a state-led investment recovery from the depression of the memorandum years. While Marxism would serve as an analytical framework, he argued, the economic policy would draw more upon Keynes, but a more radical version of the British economist than the limited reading of his *General Theory* that Varoufakis, among many others, had deployed.

Responding to that interview the British Marxist economist Michael Roberts, while acknowledging the straitjacket the euro imposed, questioned whether Greece could, by leaving and pursuing fairly conventional Keynesian policies, indeed escape the crisis. He pointed out the limitations of seeing, for example, the experience of Argentina, which broke the link between its currency and the dollar in 2001, as a model for Greece leaving the European Monetary Union:

> [The] recovery in real incomes in Argentina after the 2001 crisis was more to do with the debt default and the recovery in profitability of Argentine capital ... And the apparent success of the Argentine case was short-lived at best ... [T]he Argentine economy is back in crisis, despite Keynesian policies adopted by the government. There has been a 6 per cent fall in per capita GDP since 2011.[51]

As fruitful as the *economic* debate among Marxists is about the relevance of Marx and Keynes to elaborating policies to escape austerity, it was overshadowed by the *political* logic of the crisis in Greece. What that forced on much of the radical left in July 2015 was an increasing recognition that an alternative to the government's deal with the Troika would have to go further than merely a policy of being prepared to rupture with the euro. Events had confirmed the analysis that it was not possible for Greece to pursue an anti-austerity policy while remaining in the eurozone. But what was the left's positive alternative? That was the question which Tsipras hammered at again and again in the weeks following his signing up to the Brussels agreement.

Rupture

In the early hours of 16 July the Greek parliament passed the first of a series of 'prior actions', austerity measures demanded of Greece even before negotiations were to open up over the summer on a third bailout and memorandum. The parties of the old order voted with the government. There was no danger of the bill not passing. But the parliamentary debate and vote saw a big rebellion among Syriza MPs. In all, 32 voted against, six abstained and one was not present. Among those voting against were Varoufakis, Zoe Konstantopoulou and Panagiotis Lafazanis, along with other government ministers belonging to the Left Platform of Syriza. All 13 MPs of ANEL voted with the government. For all their bluster about 'standing up for the nation against Berlin' they voted solidly along the lines Greek big business had demanded. Before the vote 109 members of Syriza's Central Committee (out of 201) had signed a statement opposing the deal. That majority opposition was not reflected in the parliamentary group. Despite the democratic culture of the party, in government the pressures of conventional parliamentary management asserted themselves.

Nevertheless, the rebellion by 39 MPs meant that the governing coalition was reduced to just 123 MPs voting with it. It had further lost its majority in parliament. It also brought it perilously close to the 120 constitutional minimum for a minority administration to govern. Two days later Tsipras sacked those left ministers who had rebelled. ANEL was rewarded with an extra ministerial position. Its over-representation in the government was increased. But opinion polls in late July showed ANEL's popular support had slumped to under 3 per cent. The government could command large majorities in parliament for further austerity. But its base in society was weakening.

Syriza was still comfortably first – thanks to the ongoing crisis of New Democracy and of Pasok. Tsipras, too, remained popular – though there was an increase in those who held a negative opinion of him and of the government's handling of the economic crisis. What had decidedly gone that night, as teargas forced thousands of left-wing protesters against the deal to evacuate Syntagma Square, was the initial optimism of the election victory in January. As Tsipras and defenders of signing the deal sought to stem left opposition they turned to the kind of conventional arguments which Syriza voters had rejected over the previous three years.

In the debate on the second round of 'prior actions' on 22 July, Tsakalotos responded to opposition MPs who made much of the fact that the government was proposing 900 pages of measures it said it did not believe in (but had been forced into) by saying: 'You have no business making that argument, because that's exactly what you said when you did the same as we are doing now.' That was true. But the Syriza finance minister's argument made him sound little different from the kind of kindergarten exchanges which had characterised Pasok and New Democracy over the years. It was a far cry from the radically different politics which the base of Syriza still hoped for and which Tsakalotos had written about.

Tsipras's arguments against the left also relied increasingly on the old political conventions. On 21 July, the day before the second 'prior actions' vote, he told the centre-left *Ta Nea*:

> If some people believe that the alternative left project is Schäuble's plan, seizing the stock of ECB notes [from the printing house of the national mint], or giving pensioners IOUs instead of pensions, then let them go and explain that to the Greek people and not hide behind the safety of my authority.

The right-wing media had run a scaremongering campaign over an internal meeting of the left a week earlier which had, as such meetings do, canvassed various hypothetical measures – for instance those Varoufakis had revealed had been discussed by the inner cabinet. That Tsipras was prepared to use the themes of a right-wing attack on the left, in and outside Syriza, indicated the depths of the political rupture which had taken place. The leading group around him briefed that they were preparing for a showdown with the left at a special conference after the summer, to be followed by a snap election. Under Greek electoral law, party leaderships have additional power over the selection of candidates if there is less than 12 months between one general election and the next. Anonymous government sources told journalists that patience was wearing thin with the speaker of parliament. New Democracy and Pasok trailed a no confidence vote in Konstantopoulou, which required 50 MPs to table it and 151 to pass.

The sharpness of Tsipras's turn against the left, combined with how the revolt in the party over the deal had found only diluted expression in the parliamentary fraction, severely qualified, to say the least, the claim that Syriza was a party of a radically 'new type'. There were, for sure, some significant differences between it and the tired European social democratic parties. The vigorous campaign inside its branches and structures against the deal, which developed in July, testified to that. The night the second prior actions were voted through the now former energy minister Lafazanis told journalists outside parliament:

Everything went fine. Syriza is united with its differentiations. And this is how Syriza always was. How it is. And how it will continue to be in the future. Differences do not undermine the cohesion of Syriza. Differences are part of our constitution and norms of how we function.

And these differences need to be respected by everyone. These differentiations are a strength of Syriza and not a weakness. They are not an Achilles heel. Differentiations are vital and are a strength for a party of the radical left in order for it to go forward.

Time would tell how respecting of internal differences the Tsipras leadership would prove to be. No sooner had those measures passed than hardliners in the Troika began demanding yet more, even before talks on an actual bailout might begin.

That Syriza had been characterised by a large degree of pluralism is beyond doubt. It retained a coalitional feel even after it was transformed into a party with greater centralisation in 2013. But there was no escaping the fact that the concentration of power in the leadership around Tsipras, who became elected directly by the conference and not via the much broader Central Committee delegating its authority to him, allowed it an increasing autonomy and executive power of initiative. In those circumstances, pluralism could just as well be invoked by the right of the party as the left, but to justify a course of action lacking in democratic legitimacy inside the party. To some extent, that was shown by the way that Tsipras had run the government from January. It comprised a powerful inner core, with parcels of ministerial authority distributed to a plurality of different strands. The Greek constitution, like the British one, confers a lot of power on the office of prime minister.

So – the human rights lawyers got justice and immigration; the leader of the left got energy and production (as had the late Tony Benn in the British Labour government of 1974–9); finance and economics remained tightly aligned to the prime minister and his deputy – also an economist; the right-wing nationalists got defence; the centre-left patriots got foreign affairs; the tutor to senior police officers got policing; the man who had helped bring Greece into the single currency and had served as a New Democracy finance minister stayed on at the central bank …

While the right in government were allowed frequently to overstep their ministerial boundaries – the ministers of defence and of foreign affairs, for example, made programmatic speeches which undermined the policy of the minister for immigration – the left was often boxed in. The right-wing media was quick to seize upon briefings against left-wing ministers emanating from the government inner circle.

It would be a mistake, however, to seek the explanation for the defeat of the left Syriza dissidents over the Brussels deal in July in some 'iron law of oligarchy', whereby parties in government are destined to succumb to a leadership assuming power for itself and then manipulating the democratic structures. Nor do glib explanations based upon personal integrity or sincerity of belief – of a commitment to the ideas and thinking of the left – work. Alexis Tsipras is no Tony Blair. He lives modestly. He named his young son Ernesto, the first name of Che Guevara, a symbol of revolutionary and socialist integrity. While Keynes is the main economic reference point for Varoufakis, who opposed the Brussels deal, for Tsakalotos, who signed it, Marx is more the guide to economic and political analysis. The weight of the explanation for the Syriza government's capitulation in early July is, instead, to be found in the strategic dilemmas posed by trying to break with austerity capitalism.

The strategic divergence

Tsipras put a set of arguments to critics on the left. They go to the heart of the knot of strategic issues running through this book. Resting upon six months of negotiations and on the Oxi referendum revolt he challenged all those who believed that it was possible to get a better deal within the euro. For those committed to a strategy of reforming the euro and EU his case was unassailable, even if it was somewhat self-immolating – what the capitulation to the Troika showed was that it was impossible to reform the eurozone out of its inherent austerity and neoliberal, embedded bias and ideology. He unleashed a different barrage against the minority of the left which argued for leaving the euro.

First, he equated what the left was arguing for with the threat made by Wolfgang Schäuble of a punitive expulsion of Greece from the eurozone.[52] That the term Grexit was frequently used to describe both the position of Schäuble and the very different position of the left certainly assisted Tsipras in his polemic. He seized also on occasional statements by some left figures to the effect that Greece should have accepted Schäuble's plan for leaving the eurozone when it was offered.

Second, he issued a fundamental challenge to the left. To left critics inside Syriza he asked, 'Are you prepared to bring down the government? If so, what is your governmental alternative?' As we have seen, the only possible alternative in the parliament elected in January 2015 would be a government including the old parties and the centre left, which were wholly signed up to austerity. If elections are your answer, he continued, then you should be honest and stand on your own policies and platform, not hide behind mine. While it is true that the left could reasonably argue that the government had broken the democratically agreed election platform promising to curb austerity at home, the government could equally maintain that nowhere in the party's policy was a pledge to leave the euro. That impossible triangle of forces – opposing austerity but committing to stay in the euro – had indeed been a contradiction at the heart of Syriza's programme and strategy. No amount of creative ambiguity along the lines of 'we must overturn austerity whether in or out of the euro' could evade the remorseless political logic. That had been essentially the position of Tsakalotos. It collapsed into voting through a new austerity deal.

As argument raged in and outside Syriza over the summer parts of the left did articulate a credible answer to Tsipras's challenge. It began by arguing that something more profound than even the necessary rupture from the euro had been exposed by the strategic impasse the government had reached.

First, the radical and anti-capitalist response emphasised that the government's defeat in Europe was a product of its failure to confront domestic capitalist interests, for whom the institutions and other governments of the eurozone had gone into battle when the Greek parties of the old order suffered such comprehensive defeat in January. The starting point was not the so-called Grexit. It was to take the measures such as bank nationalisation and repudiating the unpayable debt, without which there could be no economic rescue for working-class Greece.[53] That would, indeed, necessitate a rupture with the euro and European institutions. But the costs of that were to be thrown onto big business, such as the shipping owners, who account for half the EU merchant fleet but whose profits are taxed at a lower rate than seamen's wages, thanks to an explicit clause in the Greek constitution.

Second, it answered the charge from Tsipras that there was no support for such a policy, and no means of implementing it, by referring back to the waves of social struggle which had brought Syriza to power in the first placed. The latest mass movement in society had been the Oxi revolt. Before the referendum, the right had tried both to scare people into voting Yes – by claiming that a No vote would mean a chaotic exit from the euro – and also to claim that it would be meaningless because people did not know what they were voting for. Having rejected those arguments before the vote, afterwards Tsipras and his supporters ended up echoing them by claiming there was no clear mandate from the referendum. Despite the sophistry, the meaning of the massive No was clear – it was a defiant rejection of the Troika. It had not listened. Instead, it had forced the Greek government to back down. One argument from the anti-capitalist left was that stronger instruments than the ballot box would now have to be deployed to break the memorandum in practice. There had already been a one-day general strike called by the ADEDY public sector trade union federation on the day the deal was voted through parliament. 'You have to understand,' a leading Syriza trade unionist at the port of Piraeus told me:

> Most of the port is still in public hands. That's despite the previous memorandums. Just because they pass something in parliament does not mean it happens out here. We have rebuilt the union

over the last two years. And we are not going to allow ourselves to be privatised.

Third, it took up Tsipras's attempt to trap the left inside the logic of the parliament elected in January by arguing that the left, in and outside Syriza, should articulate this anti-capitalist programme in the course of the anticipated battles over implementing whatever memorandum might be negotiated over the summer. The strategic dead-end the government had hit had produced both a surrender to the Troika, but also a radicalisation at the base of Syriza towards a more explicitly anti-capitalist policy and necessary rupture with the institutions of big business, Greek and European.

Recovering the thread

Exactly six months in to the Syriza government the debates about the way out of the labyrinth of austerity were much more intense than back in January. The July deal had brought a serious strategic defeat for the left in government and therefore, by extension, for the left as a whole. It was felt outside Greece, among all those who were struggling against austerity policies, particularly inside the movements of solidarity with the resistance in Greece which had erupted throughout the month of June. Yet, remarkably, the locus of the debates remained on the radical left – the right had little breathing space. In part, that's because the old governmental parties of the centre left and centre right – in Greece and across Europe – continued to suffer from a growing crisis of legitimacy, which had begun well before the 2008 economic crash. It was also testimony to a far from exhausted seam of social resistance to austerity in Greece. Elsewhere, including in Germany, there were significant echoes of that process also.

The debate in Greece was across the whole of the left – within Syriza, the Antarsya anti-capitalist coalition, inside the KKE, where the disconnect between its members and leadership was becoming more acute, and inside the trade unions and social movements. The precise political and organisational conclusions would emerge only in the course of the struggles which everyone expected to come soon. Whether they would be successful would depend on navigating further forks in the road. It was not possible literally to revisit the moments of decision which had led to the Brussels surrender. But it was both possible and necessary to retrace those steps, the better to learn from the bitter experience.

This book was written as a contribution to that process. In the myth of Theseus, after killing the Minotaur at the centre of the labyrinth the hero exits by following the thread he had unspooled during his descent. What I have tried to highlight throughout these pages is a thread running through the victories and defeats of the radical left and social movements in Greece over the last five years.

It may be summed up thus: the truly radical advances have not merely been the growth of political forces with more left-wing policies. They have not even been that voters have been prepared to look to the left in unprecedented numbers. Those are both very great gains. But the truly radical developments have been when collective, mass movements have begun to answer the very political problems they pose. In so doing, they have pointed to a radically different form of politics and strategy for change. To borrow a phrase from 167 years ago, they have reminded us that nothing is more radical than 'the independent movement of the immense majority in the interests of the immense majority'.[54]

Notes

Unless otherwise stated, direct quotes are from the author's journalistic notes.

1. From the Preface to the *Communist Manifesto* by Karl Marx and Frederick Engels, published in 1848.
2. The names of two of those camps – Sabra and Shatila – send a chill down the spine of every Palestinian. It was there in September 1982 that the fascist Falange, under the watchful eye of the Israeli army, slaughtered 5,000 unarmed women, children and, largely old, men.
3. Two terms used by participants to describe how Alexis Tsipras was treated in the Brussels negotiations in the second week of July 2015.
4. I am indebted to my friend Milena Buyum Jackson for cutting through some cynical and knowing left commentary about this initiative and reminding me of its positive social significance, and to her and Phil for how they built upon it.
5. I helped out with the Europe Says Oxi (No) collective of young activists who managed to create the online #thisisacoup phenomenon, which forced the European media to take note of the fact that there was a great deal of opposition across the continent to Merkel and the Troika. There were some learned disquisitions among the older left about why what happened was not a coup but rather a capitulation by the Greek government. While that is true, these authors missed the fundamental truth – some hundreds of thousands of people *did* something via the online initiative. That meant that large numbers of them were then open to why they should side with those in Greece who rejected the deal Tsipras signed up to and who were prepared to fight on.
6. 'Chauvinist' is used in this book in its original sense of 'aggressive or exaggerated patriotim'.
7. See Thanasis Kampagiannis, 'On the Trial of Golden Dawn', *Socialism from Below*, March 2015. Kampagiannis is one of the lawyers of the Jail Golden Dawn initiative representing the anti-fascist movement in the trial of Golden Dawn as a criminal organisation.
8. This is the combined total for the left as a whole.

9. I use the term 'orthodox' to distinguish the traditional, pro-Moscow strand of the Communist tradition from what became known as Eurocommunism in the 1970s.

10. His daughter, Zoe Konstantopoulou was to become a Syriza MP in 2012 and then, in 2015, speaker of the parliament and prominent party dissident in the splits which emerged over the third memorandum.

11. DEA, the Internationalist Workers' Left, a Trotskyist organisation in Syriza, resisted such dissolution of its structures, and KOE, the Communist Organisation of Greece, a Maoist organisation, also put up some opposition.

12. The presidency in Greece is often described as a largely symbolic office. In strict constitutional terms that is true. But as later events were to prove, the public profile afforded by the position allows for considerable intervention in politics.

13. Christos Laskos and Euclid Tsakalotos, *Crucible of Resistance*, London, Pluto Press, 2013.

14. See: David Bell and David Blanchflower, 'Youth Unemployment in Greece: Measuring the Challenge', *IZA Journal of European Labor Studies* 4(1). Available at http://www.izajoels.com/content/4/1/1

15. Bell and Blanchflower, 'Youth Unemployment ...'.

16. Bell and Blanchflower, 'Youth Unemployment ...'.

17. See: http://news.bbc.co.uk/2/hi/europe/4763777.stm

18. See 'Cities Need Cleaning Up: Samaras', *Kathimerini*, 20 April 2012.

19. See 'UN Rapporteur Criticises Migrant Detention Conditions', *Kathimerini*, 3 December 2012.

20. Interview with author.

21. At the time he was junior economics minister; he was later promoted to cabinet ranking minister of finance.

22. It would be entirely legal to convert the special shares of the Greek state in the banking system into ordinary shares, thus making the state the majority shareholder.

23. 'Greece Must Reform Says Central Bank Governor', *Wall Street Journal*, 26 February.

24. As we have seen on p. 55, this was an additional source of confusion for the left seeking to relate to the movement of the squares in 2011, which copied the earlier Spanish example and called itself the *aganaktismenoi*, after the *indignados*, the indignant ones.

25. This exclusion was more extreme than the *Berufsverbot* in West Germany and similar Cold War measures in other countries barring Communists from certain categories of employment.

26. See: http://greece.greekreporter.com/2015/03/07/greek-foreign-minister-jihadists-will-flock-in-europe-if-greece-crumbles/#sthash.bKnxMJ5Y.dpuf

27. See Ahmet Davutoglu, *Strategic Depth*, first published in Turkish as *Stratejik Derenlik*, Istanbul: Kure Yayinlari, 2009.

28. See: www.mfa.gr/en/current-affairs/news-announcements/foreign-ministry-announcement-on-the-terrorist-attacks-in-egypts-sinai-peninsula.html and other foreign ministry bulletins.

29. See: http://carnegie.ru/eurasiaoutlook/?fa=59768

30. See: www.hurriyetdailynews.com/nato-sings-we-are-the-world-for-peace-during-antalya-meeting.aspx?pageID=238&nID=82392&NewsCatID=359

31. See: http://en.enikos.gr/society/26144,Greek-Special-Forces-slogans-chanted-during-parade-prompt-backlash.html

32. See: Yannis Panoussis, 'Media, Crime and Criminal Justice', in L.K. Cheliotis and S. Xenakis (eds) *Crime and Punishment in Contemporary Greece*, New York: Peter Lang, 2011.

33. 'Greece's Leader Warns Merkel of "Impossible" Debt Repayments', *Financial Times*, 22 April 2015.

34. 'Misguided Attacks', *Kathimerini*, 13 May 2015.

35. Labour Party Annual Conference Report, 1976.

36. An expression I coined after a leading To Potami MP told a television audience that 'the poor make wrong choices in moments of economic crisis'.

37. 'Frustrated Officials Want Greek Premier to Ditch Syriza Far Left', *Financial Times*, 5 April 2015.

38. 'US Ambassador in Warning Over Terrorist Release', *Greek Reporter*, 19 April 2015.

39. Banks being banks, they found a way further to restrict that allowance. For the next three weeks of bank closures we were told that there was for some reason a shortage of smaller notes in Greece. So it was possible to withdraw a single €50 note, but not three €20s or six €10s. At a stroke the bankers reduced the daily limit by 17 per cent.

40. For an early criticism of this sort see K. Ovenden, 'Europe: The Bosses' Fading Star?', *Socialist Review*, July/August 1997.

41. John Milios, 'The Class Logic behind Austerity Policies in the Euro-Area: Can SYRIZA Put Forward a Progressive Alternative?', June 2015, http://www.globalresearch.ca/the-class-logic-behind-austerity-policies-in-the-euro-area-can-syriza-put-forward-a-progressive-alternative/5452673

42. I intend to return to such an examination in later work.

43. Yanis Varoufakis, *The Global Minotaur*, London: Zed Books, 2011, p. 198.

44. Yanis Varoufakis, Stuart Holland and James K. Galbraith, 'A Modest Proposal for Resolving the Eurozone Crisis', Version 4.0, July 2013, https://varoufakis.files.wordpress.com/2013/07/a-modest-proposal-for-resolving-the-eurozone-crisis-version-4-0-final1.pdf.

45. See: www.newstatesman.com/world-affairs/2015/07/exclusive-yanis-varoufakis-opens-about-his-five-month-battle-save-greece

46. 'Tapes Reveal Varoufakis Plan B', *Kathimerini*, 26 July 2015.

47. Christos Laskos and Euclid Tsakalotos, *Crucible of Resistance*, London, Pluto Press, 2013.

48. Euclid Tsakalotos, 'A European Solution to the Crisis?', http://www.chronosmag.eu/index.php/e-tsakalotos-a-european-solution-to-the-crisis.html

49. Costas Lapavitsas et al., *Crisis in the Eurozone*, London: Verso, 2012.

50. See: https://www.jacobinmag.com/2015/03/lapavitsas-varoufakis-grexit-syriza/

51. See: https://thenextrecession.wordpress.com/2015/03/14/greece-keynes-or-marx/. Mine is a cursory examination of an involved debate. A full treatment of it would have to take account of the evolution of various positions in the course of the Syriza experience. In any case, my central point is that, whatever the differences at the level of economic theory, they were over-ridden by the logic of the political conflict between Greece and the Troika.

52. This threat was still being brandished as this book was at the printers.

53. In a widely reported speech, Costas Lapavitsas outlined the case forcefully at the 'Democracy Rising' Conference in Athens on 18 July 2015.

54. Karl Marx and Frederick Engels, *The Communist Manifesto*.

Published in association with

philosophy**football**●com

sporting outfitters of intellectual distinction

What business do self-styled 'sporting outfitters of intellectual distinction' have in putting our logo on a book about current Greek politics? Syriza's January election campaign was something that inspired us. We rushed out a T-shirt in support, and used the funds raised to generate practical solidarity. Kevin Ovenden was an old friend of ours, he'd organised the Viva Palestina convoys to break the siege of Gaza which we'd also supported. We'd kitted out all the drivers and crews, provided the vehicle graphics, and Hugh, Philosophy Football's co-founder, drove one of the vehicles all the way to Gaza too.

In January 2015 we paid for Kevin to be based in Athens for four weeks covering the election, with his reports provided free of charge to radical media in Britain, the USA, Australia and Serbia. This superb book developed out of these reports. We also funded Kevin's return to Athens to complete it. Other companies sell T-shirts, good luck to them. We're proud to say that we prefer to trade in ideas and ideals, the shirt a canvass for both, and a platform for just this kind of initiative. If you want to know more, visit www.philosophyfootball.com or follow us @phil_football.